# LAKE GARDA

## Travel Guide

**Explore the Beauty, Culture, and Hidden Gems of Italy's Majestic Lake Region**

James D. Vollmer

# TABLE OF CONTENT

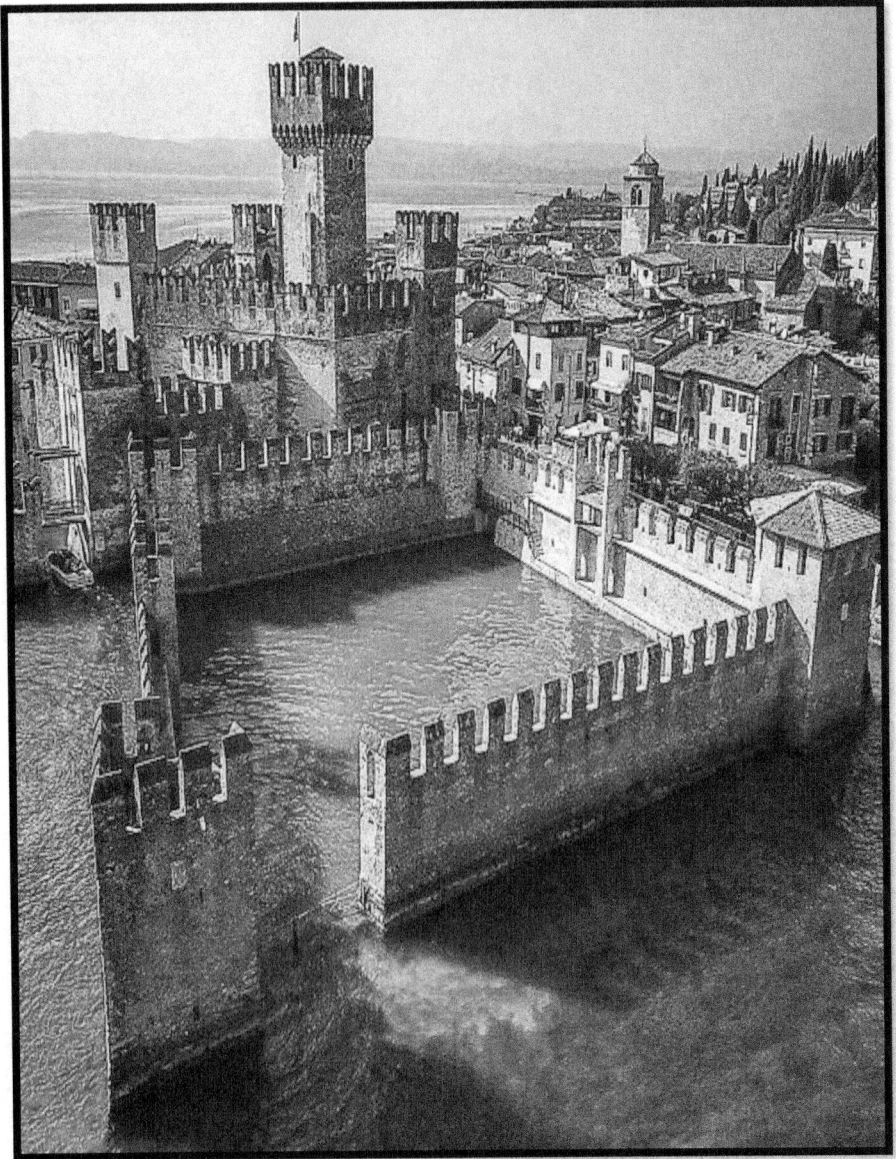

# CHAPTER 1: DISCOVERING LAKE GARDA

## Introduction to Lake Garda

L ake Garda is a destination that surprises travelers with its diversity. It's the largest lake in Italy, stretching across three regions—Lombardy, Veneto, and Trentino-Alto Adige—each contributing something distinct to its character. From the charming medieval towns along the shoreline to the dramatic mountain backdrops, every corner of Lake Garda feels different from the last.

People come here for many reasons. Some want to see the historical sites that have stood for centuries. Others look for outdoor activities, taking advantage of the hiking trails, water sports, and cycling routes that make this region a playground for adventure. Then there are those who simply want to relax, soaking in the views with a glass of local wine in hand. Whatever the reason, Lake Garda has a way of drawing people in and making them want to stay longer than planned.

The lake has been a source of inspiration for poets, artists, and writers for centuries. It was a favorite of Goethe, who wrote about it in his Italian Journey, and its shores have welcomed travelers seeking peace and inspiration for generations. Today, it continues to offer that same sense of escape, balancing natural beauty with a deep cultural heritage that makes it more than just a scenic stop on an itinerary.

## Geographical Insights

Lake Garda is the largest lake in Italy, spanning approximately 370 square kilometers, and is situated in the northern part of the country. It stretches across three regions—Lombardy to the west, Veneto to the east, and Trentino-Alto Adige to the north—each contributing to its diverse landscape and cultural influences. The lake's elongated shape runs from north to south, with a narrow, fjord-like northern end framed by towering mountains, while the southern section widens into a gentler, rolling landscape. This contrast between the north and south significantly impacts the climate, local culture, and the type of experiences visitors can expect.

The northern end of Lake Garda is dominated by the dramatic peaks of the Italian Alps and the Dolomites. Here, the lake is deep, its waters plunging to over 340 meters in some areas, and the steep cliffs create a striking visual contrast against the blue waters. Towns like Riva del Garda, Torbole, and Malcesine are nestled at the foot of these mountains, creating a postcard-worthy scene that has drawn travelers for centuries. The geography here lends itself to outdoor adventure—windsurfing, sailing, and rock climbing are particularly popular, thanks to the strong winds that sweep through this part of the lake.

One of the defining geographical features of the northern section is the presence of the Monte Baldo mountain range. Rising to over 2,200 meters, Monte Baldo is often referred to as the "Garden of Europe" due to its rich biodiversity. The mountain is home to a variety of plant species, some of which are found nowhere else in the world. A cable car from Malcesine takes visitors up to the summit, where they are greeted with sweeping panoramic views of the lake and surrounding valleys. Hiking trails crisscross the mountain, offering paths suitable for both beginners and experienced trekkers.

Moving south, the landscape gradually softens. The steep cliffs and rugged mountains give way to rolling hills and fertile plains. This transition is noticeable when traveling through towns like Limone sul Garda and Gargnano, where the terrain becomes more accommodating to agriculture. Olive groves and vineyards begin to dominate the scenery, and the Mediterranean influence becomes more apparent. The air is warmer, the flora is more diverse, and citrus trees thrive in the milder climate.

The southern portion of Lake Garda, where towns like Sirmione, Desenzano del Garda, and Peschiera del Garda are located, is characterized by a broader expanse of water and a gentler shoreline. Unlike the north, where the mountains descend dramatically into the lake, the south is marked by a flatter, more open terrain. This difference in geography has influenced the development of the towns here—while the northern settlements are compact and built into the landscape, the southern towns have broader promenades, spacious piazzas, and larger beaches.

One of the most famous geographical features of the southern lake is the Sirmione Peninsula, which extends into the water like a thin finger. This narrow strip of land is home to the town of Sirmione, known for its medieval Scaliger Castle and the ancient Roman ruins of the Grottoes of Catullus. The peninsula's unique position in the lake makes it one of the most scenic spots in the region, offering stunning views in every direction.

The lake itself is fed by the Sarca River, which flows in from the north, and drained by the Mincio River in the south. This continuous flow helps maintain the lake's clarity and freshness, making it one of the cleanest bodies of water in Italy. The water temperature varies depending on the season, with summer temperatures reaching around 20-25°C, making it ideal for swimming and water activities.

Another notable feature of Lake Garda is its islands. The largest, Isola del Garda, lies off the western shore near San Felice del Benaco. Privately owned but open for guided tours, this island is home to a stunning Venetian-style villa and lush gardens. Other islands, such as Isola San Biagio and Isola dei Conigli, offer more secluded spots for visitors looking to escape the mainland crowds.

The climate around Lake Garda varies significantly depending on the location. The northern end, due to its mountainous surroundings, experiences cooler temperatures, especially in winter, when the peaks are often dusted with snow. The southern end, on the other hand, enjoys a much milder, Mediterranean-style climate, with warm summers and relatively mild winters. This geographical variation makes Lake Garda a year-round destination—while summer brings sun-seekers and water sports enthusiasts, spring and autumn attract hikers, cyclists, and those looking for a more relaxed experience.

The lake's unique geographical makeup also influences the local cuisine. The fertile lands around the southern and western shores produce some of Italy's best olive oil, known for its delicate and slightly peppery flavor. Vineyards around Bardolino and Lugana create wines that pair perfectly with the region's dishes, from freshwater fish to handmade pasta. Meanwhile, the northern towns, influenced by their Alpine surroundings, incorporate heartier ingredients like polenta, mountain cheeses, and game meats into their traditional recipes.

## The Unique Charm of Lake Garda

Lake Garda has a distinctive character that sets it apart from any other destination in Italy. Its charm is woven from a combination of breathtaking landscapes, rich history, diverse local cultures, and an atmosphere that balances tranquility with vibrant energy. From the dramatic cliffs of the northern shore to the sun-drenched vineyards in the south, every corner of the lake offers something different yet equally captivating.

One of the first things that strikes visitors about Lake Garda is the sheer variety of its scenery. The northern end of the lake, surrounded by towering mountains, has a rugged and almost Alpine feel, while the southern shores exude a Mediterranean ambiance with their rolling hills, olive groves, and cypress trees. This geographical contrast makes the lake feel like several destinations in one. Visitors can start their day hiking in the crisp mountain air of Riva del Garda and end it sipping wine on a terrace in the warm glow of a Sirmione sunset.

The lake's charm is also deeply rooted in its history, which spans thousands of years. Ancient Romans were among the first to recognize its beauty, building luxurious villas along its shores. The ruins of one such villa, the Grottoes of Catullus in Sirmione, stand as a testament to their love for this idyllic setting. Medieval castles, like the Scaliger Castles in Malcesine and Sirmione, add a fairytale-like element to the landscape. The lake has also played a role in various historical conflicts, from medieval battles to its strategic importance during World War II. Walking through the old town centers, where centuries-old buildings house modern cafés and boutiques, creates a fascinating blend of past and present.

Each town around Lake Garda has its own personality, adding to the region's allure. Riva del Garda, with its elegant piazzas and alpine backdrop, feels different from the relaxed, lemon-scented streets of Limone sul Garda. Malcesine, perched at the foot of Monte Baldo, is defined by its medieval castle and winding lanes, while Desenzano del Garda, the lake's largest town, has a lively energy with its bustling harbor, fashionable shops, and vibrant nightlife. Bardolino and Lazise, on the eastern shore, are known for their wines and relaxed lakefront promenades, while Salò, on the western side, boasts grand architecture and a sophisticated atmosphere.

Another aspect of Lake Garda's charm is its timeless appeal. While other Italian destinations might feel overwhelmingly touristy, the lake maintains a balance between being a beloved getaway and a place where locals continue their daily lives. Markets selling fresh produce, small family-run trattorias, and traditional festivals ensure that the local culture remains strong. This authenticity is part of what draws visitors back year after year—there's always something familiar, yet new discoveries await at every turn.

The lake's microclimate contributes to its unique atmosphere. Thanks to its protective mountains and vast body of water, Lake Garda enjoys a relatively mild climate throughout the year. In spring, wildflowers bloom along the hillsides, making it an ideal time for hiking and cycling. Summer brings long, warm days perfect for swimming, sailing, or simply relaxing on a lakeside terrace. Autumn sees the vineyards and olive groves come to life with harvest season, offering some of the best food and wine experiences. Even in winter, the lake remains charming, with snow-capped mountains in the background and a peaceful ambiance that is far removed from the busier months.

The culinary traditions of Lake Garda also contribute to its distinct charm. The region produces some of Italy's best olive oil, thanks to the mild climate and mineral-rich soil. Wines from the Bardolino and Lugana regions are highly regarded, and local dishes showcase fresh lake fish, handmade pasta, and seasonal ingredients. Whether it's a lakeside dinner in a Michelin-starred restaurant or a casual meal in a rustic osteria, food is an essential part of the Lake Garda experience.

The lake's ability to offer both relaxation and adventure is another reason why it continues to captivate visitors. Those looking for a peaceful retreat can find it in the quiet coves and scenic gardens, while adrenaline seekers can take advantage of the lake's famous winds for windsurfing and sailing. Cyclists have access to world-class trails, ranging from scenic lakeside routes to challenging mountain paths. The ability to tailor an experience to different moods and interests makes Lake Garda a destination that appeals to all kinds of travelers.

At sunset, when the water reflects the changing colors of the sky and the lights from the lakeside villages begin to twinkle, it's easy to understand why Lake Garda has enchanted visitors for centuries. It's not just a destination—it's an experience that lingers long after leaving, calling travelers back time and time again.

# First Impressions

The moment of arrival at Lake Garda is something travelers remember vividly. Whether coming by car, train, or ferry, the first glimpse of the lake is often breathtaking. The shimmering blue water, framed by mountains or rolling hills, creates an instant sense of tranquility. The air carries a freshness that blends Alpine crispness with Mediterranean warmth, a reflection of the region's unique climate. Every visitor's first impression is shaped by the route they take, the season of their visit, and the town where they begin their journey. But no matter the entry point, one thing remains constant—Lake Garda immediately captivates.

## Arriving at Lake Garda

How you arrive at Lake Garda influences your initial experience. Many visitors first see the lake from the window of a train or car, catching sight of its glistening waters as they approach from Verona, Milan, or Venice. Others arrive by ferry, watching as the shoreline gradually unfolds, revealing historic villages and steep cliffs. Each arrival method offers a unique introduction to the lake's charm.

### 🚌 By Car: The Scenic Drive In

For many, driving to Lake Garda is the first true experience of the region's beauty. The roads leading to the lake vary dramatically depending on the direction of approach. From the south, highways pass through vineyard-covered hills and olive groves, gradually revealing the lake as a vast expanse of blue. Arriving from the north is a different experience altogether, as the road winds through towering mountains before suddenly opening up to breathtaking views of the lake below.

Driving along the lake itself is an adventure. The famous **Gardesana** road, which circles the entire lake, is a masterpiece of engineering, hugging cliffs, weaving through tunnels, and offering spectacular panoramic views. Towns appear suddenly, their medieval towers and pastel-colored buildings adding charm to the journey. Whether entering from the bustling southern towns or the dramatic northern landscapes, the drive into Lake Garda sets the tone for what's to come.

### 🚊 By Train: A Smooth and Scenic Approach

For those arriving by train, the first view of the lake is just as enchanting. The main railway stations serving Lake Garda— Desenzano del Garda and Peschiera del Garda—are located on the southern shore. As the train approaches, travelers catch glimpses of the water, the distant mountains, and the small harbors lined with fishing boats. Stepping off the train, the air feels different—warmer in summer, fresh in spring, with a distinct scent of lake water and citrus trees. From the station, it's easy to hop on a ferry or bus to reach other lakeside towns.

### 🚢 By Ferry: A Grand Entrance on the Water

Arriving by ferry offers one of the most memorable introductions to Lake Garda. Many visitors take a boat from one of the larger towns, such as Desenzano or Riva del Garda, and let the lake itself reveal its secrets. The ferry glides past castle-topped cliffs, colorful villages, and rocky outcrops where cypress trees grow in clusters. As the boat docks, the sounds of lapping waves mix with the chatter from lakeside cafés, immediately immersing visitors in the lake's peaceful rhythm.

### ✈ By Air: A Quick Gateway to the Lake

For international travelers, the journey often begins at **Verona Villafranca Airport**, the closest airport to Lake Garda. From here, it's a short drive or train ride to the southern shores. Milan's airports— Malpensa, Linate, and Bergamo—are also common entry points, offering slightly longer but still scenic journeys to the lake. Landing in Italy and heading straight for Lake Garda is a smooth transition from travel mode to relaxation.

Regardless of how one arrives, the first impression of Lake Garda is striking. The lake's vastness, its varying landscapes, and the balance between nature and history create an immediate sense of wonder.

## Scenic Landscapes and Natural Beauty

The landscape surrounding Lake Garda is nothing short of spectacular. The lake itself stretches over 50 kilometers from north to south, offering an ever-changing backdrop of mountains, rolling hills, and charming villages. The way the scenery shifts along its shores is one of its most striking features.

### The Northern Majesty: Mountains and Cliffs

The northern end of Lake Garda is where the landscape is most dramatic. Towering limestone cliffs rise steeply from the water, creating a fjord-like effect. The peaks of Monte Baldo dominate the skyline, providing an ever-present reminder of the region's Alpine character. This part of the lake is particularly stunning at sunrise, when the first light catches the rugged cliffs, casting golden reflections onto the water.

Towns like Riva del Garda and Limone sul Garda nestle against these cliffs, their pastel-colored buildings standing in contrast to the rocky landscape. The northern shoreline is also known for its strong winds, making it a paradise for windsurfers and sailors. Watching the colorful sails glide across the deep blue water is a sight that perfectly captures the lake's dynamic beauty.

### The Central Region: Rolling Hills and Vineyards

Moving south, the mountains give way to gentler slopes. This central stretch of the lake, home to towns like Malcesine and Garda, is defined by olive groves, vineyards, and cypress trees. The air is filled with the scent of lavender and rosemary, especially in the warmer months.

Monte Baldo, which dominates the northern view, is also accessible from this region via a cable car that ascends from Malcesine. The ride up offers some of the best panoramic views of the lake, stretching all the way to the southern shores. Hikers and cyclists often take advantage of Monte Baldo's trails, which offer sweeping vistas of the lake from above.

### The Southern Shores: Mediterranean Warmth

As the lake widens towards the south, the scenery takes on a distinctly Mediterranean feel. The rugged cliffs are replaced by gentle hills, dotted with vineyards and historic villas. This area, home to towns like Sirmione, Desenzano, and Bardolino, is known for its lush gardens, grand promenades, and thermal springs.

Sirmione, in particular, is famous for its unique location on a narrow peninsula that juts into the lake. The combination of medieval architecture, ancient Roman ruins, and crystal-clear waters gives it a dreamlike quality. The water in this part of the lake tends to be calmer, making it ideal for swimming, boating, and lakeside relaxation.

## The Ever-Changing Water

One of the most fascinating aspects of Lake Garda's natural beauty is the way its water changes color. Depending on the time of day, the weather, and the angle of the sun, the lake can appear deep blue, emerald green, or even a shimmering silver. In the early morning, a light mist often lingers over the surface, creating a mystical atmosphere. By midday, the water sparkles under the bright sun, while in the evening, the reflections of the lakeside villages cast golden hues onto its surface.

## A Haven for Outdoor Enthusiasts

Beyond its visual appeal, the landscape of Lake Garda offers endless opportunities for outdoor activities. The lake's shores are lined with walking and cycling paths, allowing visitors to appreciate its beauty at a leisurely pace. The hills and mountains provide excellent hiking routes, while the lake itself is perfect for water sports. Whether it's a quiet moment on a secluded beach, a scenic drive along the Gardesana road, or an adventure in the hills, Lake Garda's natural beauty is always present, offering new perspectives with every turn.

First-time visitors often find themselves pausing, simply to take it all in. The landscape has a way of making people slow down and appreciate the details—the way the light dances on the water, the scent of citrus trees in the breeze, or the sound of waves gently lapping against the shore. It's these small, sensory moments that leave a lasting impression, ensuring that the first encounter with Lake Garda is just the beginning of a deeper connection.

# Essential Travel Information

Planning a trip to Lake Garda involves more than just choosing where to stay and what to do. Proper preparation ensures a smooth experience, allowing you to focus on the beauty of the region without unnecessary stress. From knowing what to pack to having the right documents, getting the details right makes all the difference.

## Travel Preparation and Essentials

Before setting off for Lake Garda, taking the time to organize your belongings and paperwork will make your journey more enjoyable. The lake's diverse landscapes and varied activities call for a well-thought-out packing list, while understanding entry requirements and local regulations will help avoid unexpected issues.

### Packing Checklist

Packing for Lake Garda depends on the season, planned activities, and personal preferences. The lake's climate varies significantly between the northern and southern regions, as well as throughout the year. The right clothing, accessories, and essentials will ensure comfort in any conditions.

### Clothing for the Season

**Spring (March–May):** The weather can be unpredictable, with mild days and cooler evenings. Light layers are essential, including a sweater or light jacket for evenings. A rainproof jacket is also recommended, as spring showers are common.

**Summer (June–August):** Temperatures can soar, especially in the southern towns. Breathable fabrics, shorts, T-shirts, and dresses are best for daytime, while a light sweater may be useful for breezier evenings by the lake. Swimwear is a must for those planning to take a dip.

**Autumn (September–November):** Early autumn remains warm, but temperatures gradually drop. Layering is key, with long-sleeve shirts, a light jacket, and comfortable walking shoes for exploring.

❄ **Winter (December–February):** While the southern towns remain relatively mild, the northern areas near the mountains can be quite cold. A warm coat, gloves, and sturdy shoes are necessary, especially for those planning to visit higher-altitude locations.

## Footwear

Comfortable walking shoes are crucial. The cobbled streets in historic towns, hiking trails, and long lakeside promenades call for sturdy, well-cushioned shoes. Sandals or lightweight sneakers work well in the warmer months, while waterproof boots are ideal for winter or hiking.

## Accessories and Essentials

- ➡ Sunglasses and Sunscreen: Even in cooler months, the sun reflecting off the water can be intense.
- ➡ Reusable Water Bottle: Many towns have public fountains with drinkable water, making it easy to stay hydrated.
- ➡ Daypack or Small Backpack: Useful for carrying essentials while exploring.
- ➡ Travel Adapter: Italy uses Type F/L plugs, so bringing an adapter is necessary for visitors from countries with different socket types.
- ➡ Medications and First Aid Kit: Pharmacies are widely available, but bringing necessary prescription medications and basic first-aid supplies is advisable.

## Tech and Gadgets

- ➡ Phone and Charger: Mobile coverage is strong around the lake, and having a phone handy for maps, reservations, and translation apps is helpful.
- ➡ Power Bank: Useful for long days of sightseeing.
- ➡ Camera or Smartphone with Good Camera Quality: The landscapes and historic towns provide countless opportunities for stunning photos.
- ➡ E-Reader or Book: Perfect for relaxing by the water or passing time on train or ferry rides.

## Required Travel Documents

Preparing the right documents before a trip to Lake Garda is essential to ensure a smooth experience. Italy has specific entry requirements depending on nationality, purpose of visit, and length of stay. Understanding the necessary paperwork helps avoid last-minute complications and ensures compliance with Italian and EU regulations.

### Passport Requirements

All travelers entering Italy must have a valid passport. The passport should meet the following criteria:

➩ **Validity:** It must be valid for at least three months beyond the planned departure date from the Schengen Area. Some airlines may require six months of validity, so checking airline policies before departure is recommended.

➩ **Blank Pages:** At least one blank page is required for entry and exit stamps.

For EU, EEA, and Swiss nationals, a national identity card is sufficient for entry instead of a passport.

### Visa Regulations

Italy is part of the Schengen Area, meaning visa requirements depend on the traveler's nationality.

➩ **Visa-Free Entry:** Citizens of the **EU, EEA, Switzerland, the UK, the US, Canada, Australia, New Zealand, Japan**, and several other countries can visit Italy for up to **90 days within a 180-day period** without a visa for tourism or business purposes.

➩ **Schengen Visa:** Travelers from countries not included in the visa-free list must apply for a Schengen Visa before arrival. This visa allows stays of up to 90 days within a 180-day period and permits travel to other Schengen countries.

➩ **Visa Application Process:** Applications must be submitted at the nearest Italian consulate or embassy, usually requiring:

❖ A completed visa application form
❖ A valid passport
❖ Proof of accommodation (hotel reservation or invitation letter)
❖ Travel itinerary

❖ Travel insurance covering at least €30,000 in medical expenses
❖ Proof of financial means (such as bank statements or an employment letter)
❖ A return flight ticket or proof of onward travel

Processing times vary, so applying at least one month before the trip is advisable.

**ETIAS Travel Authorization (Starting 2025)**
From 2025, non-EU visitors from visa-exempt countries (including the US, UK, Canada, and Australia) will need to apply for an ETIAS (European Travel Information and Authorization System) approval before traveling to Italy. This is an online pre-screening system designed to enhance border security. ETIAS will be valid for **three years** and allow multiple entries for stays of up to 90 days per visit.

**Residence and Long-Stay Visas**
For those planning to stay in Italy for **more than 90 days**, a **national visa (D visa)** is required. This applies to students, workers, and those relocating for extended periods. Unlike the Schengen Visa, a national visa allows a longer stay but requires additional documentation, including proof of accommodation, financial stability, and sometimes an Italian sponsor.

**Travel Insurance Requirements**
While not always mandatory for visa-free travelers, travel insurance is highly recommended. Those applying for a Schengen Visa must provide proof of a policy covering at least €30,000 in medical expenses, including emergency hospital care and repatriation. Even for those who don't need a visa, insurance helps cover unexpected medical emergencies, trip cancellations, or lost belongings.

**Health Documentation**
➡ **COVID-19 Requirements:** Italy no longer requires COVID-19 vaccination proof or testing for entry, but travelers should check for any updates before their trip.

➪ **Routine Vaccinations:** No specific vaccinations are required for entry into Italy, but keeping up with standard immunizations (such as measles, tetanus, and hepatitis A) is recommended.

## International Driving Permit (IDP)

For those planning to rent a car in Italy, an International Driving Permit (IDP) is required for non-EU driver's license holders. EU citizens can use their national driver's license, but visitors from the US, Canada, Australia, and other non-EU countries must carry both their home country's driver's license and an IDP. This document translates the home license into multiple languages and is valid for one year.

## Entry Requirements for Minors

➪ Children under 18 must have a valid passport or an ID card (for EU citizens).

➪ If a minor is traveling alone or with only one parent, some countries require additional documents, such as a **notarized consent letter** from the absent parent(s). Italian border authorities may request this letter, so it's best to check with the airline and embassy before travel.

## Proof of Accommodation and Funds

While not always requested at the border, travelers should be prepared to provide:

➪ **Proof of stay:** Hotel reservations, an Airbnb booking, or an invitation letter if staying with family or friends.

➪ **Financial means:** Proof of sufficient funds to cover the stay, such as cash, credit cards, or bank statements. The Italian government recommends a minimum of **€50 per day per traveler**, though this may vary based on accommodation and travel plans.

## Customs and Border Regulations

Travelers arriving in Italy must comply with EU customs rules:

➪ **Duty-Free Allowances:** Personal use items and purchases within the EU are unrestricted. Non-EU travelers can bring in limited

amounts of alcohol, tobacco, and other goods without declaring them.
⇨ **Declaring Cash:** Carrying over **€10,000** in cash (or equivalent) requires a declaration at customs.

## Pet Travel Regulations
Bringing a pet to Italy requires:
⇨ An EU Pet Passport (for travelers from the EU) or an official veterinary certificate (for non-EU visitors).
⇨ Microchipping and proof of rabies vaccination at least 21 days before travel.
⇨ Certain dog breeds may have additional restrictions.
Being aware of these requirements ensures a smooth entry into Italy, allowing travelers to focus on experiencing Lake Garda without administrative hassles.

## Currency and Payment Options
Italy uses the **euro (€)** as its official currency. Banknotes come in denominations of 5, 10, 20, 50, 100, 200, and 500 euros, while coins range from 1 cent to 2 euros. Most businesses around Lake Garda accept cash and card payments, but having some euros on hand is always useful, particularly in smaller towns and for certain transactions.

### Cash and ATMs
While card payments are widely accepted in restaurants, hotels, and major shops, smaller businesses—such as family-run cafés, market stalls, or local ferries—sometimes prefer cash. ATMs, known as **bancomat,** are available in all major towns and many villages. These machines allow cash withdrawals using international debit and credit cards. It's best to check with your bank regarding international withdrawal fees before traveling.

### Credit and Debit Cards
Visa and Mastercard are the most widely accepted cards, followed by American Express and Maestro. Contactless payments are common, but it's wise to carry a backup payment option in case a business

prefers cash. Some small businesses may have a minimum spending limit for card transactions.

## Currency Exchange

Exchanging money in Italy is straightforward, with currency exchange offices located in airports, train stations, and tourist-heavy areas. Banks also offer exchange services, though they may have shorter operating hours. Exchange rates are generally more favorable when withdrawing from an ATM compared to exchanging cash at an airport or hotel.

## Mobile Payments

Apple Pay, Google Pay, and Samsung Pay are becoming increasingly popular, especially in larger towns. Many restaurants, shops, and transport services now accept mobile payments, though some rural areas may still rely more on traditional methods.

## Tipping Culture

Tipping in Italy is not as customary as in some other countries. In restaurants, service charges (**coperto**) are often included in the bill, usually ranging from 1 to 3 euros per person. If service is not included, rounding up the bill or leaving a small tip (5-10%) is appreciated but not expected. Taxi drivers, hotel staff, and tour guides may also appreciate small gratuities, but there is no strict rule.

## Internet Access and Mobile Services

Reliable internet and mobile service make staying connected at Lake Garda convenient. Wi-Fi is widely available, and mobile networks provide good coverage throughout the region, though reception may weaken in some mountainous or rural areas.

## Wi-Fi Availability

Hotels, cafés, and restaurants in tourist areas usually offer free Wi-Fi, though speeds and reliability vary. Some establishments require a password, so it's worth asking staff if access is needed. Public Wi-Fi hotspots are available in some town centers and transportation hubs, though they may have limited bandwidth.

## Mobile Networks and SIM Cards

Italy has several major mobile operators, including TIM, Vodafone, and WindTre, all of which provide strong coverage around Lake Garda. Travelers needing mobile data can either use international roaming from their home provider or purchase a local SIM card.

## Buying a Local SIM Card

For those staying in Italy for more than a few days, a local SIM card can be a cost-effective option. Prepaid SIMs with data packages are available at mobile shops, electronics stores, and even some supermarkets. Passport identification is required for purchase. Providers offer a range of plans, including short-term tourist packages with generous data allowances.

## eSIM Options

For travelers with eSIM-compatible devices, purchasing an Italian eSIM online before arrival is an alternative to physical SIM cards. These can be activated immediately, avoiding the need to visit a store.

## Roaming Charges

EU citizens can use their mobile plans in Italy without additional roaming fees. Travelers from non-EU countries should check with their providers for roaming costs, as charges can be high. Some providers offer international data plans, which may be more affordable than standard roaming fees.

## Language Basics for Travelers

Italian is the official language in Lake Garda, though English is widely spoken in tourist areas. That said, learning a few key phrases can enhance interactions and show respect for the local culture. In smaller villages and less touristy areas, basic Italian is especially useful.

## Common Greetings and Polite Expressions

- ➡ Buongiorno – Good morning
- ➡ Buonasera – Good evening
- ➡ Ciao – Hi/Bye (informal)
- ➡ Arrivederci – Goodbye
- ➡ Per favore – Please
- ➡ Grazie – Thank you
- ➡ Prego – You're welcome

⇨  Mi scusi – Excuse me / I'm sorry

## Ordering Food and Drinks
⇨  Un tavolo per due, per favore. – A table for two, please.
⇨  Il menù, per favore. – The menu, please.
⇨  Vorrei ordinare… – I would like to order…
⇨  Il conto, per favore. – The bill, please.
⇨  Acqua naturale/frizzante. – Still/sparkling water.

## Getting Around
⇨  Dov'è la stazione? – Where is the station?
⇨  Quanto costa un biglietto per…? – How much is a ticket to…?
⇨  A che ora parte il treno? – What time does the train leave?
⇨  C'è un autobus per…? – Is there a bus to…?

## Shopping and Payments
⇨  Quanto costa? – How much does it cost?
⇨  Accettate carte di credito? – Do you accept credit cards?
⇨  Posso avere lo scontrino? – Can I have the receipt?

## Emergency and Assistance
⇨  Aiuto! – Help!
⇨  Ho bisogno di un dottore. – I need a doctor.
⇨  Chiami un'ambulanza! – Call an ambulance!
⇨  Dov'è la farmacia più vicina? – Where is the nearest pharmacy?
⇨  Dov'è il bagno? – Where is the bathroom?

While English is often understood, especially in hotels and restaurants, making an effort to use simple Italian phrases can be met with appreciation. Even basic greetings and polite expressions can go a long way in creating a more enjoyable and respectful travel experience.

## Safety and Health Guidelines

Traveling to Lake Garda is generally a smooth and enjoyable experience, but being aware of safety and health considerations ensures a stress-free visit. Italy has a well-developed infrastructure, and Lake Garda's towns and villages are known for their welcoming atmosphere. Still, it's always wise to be prepared for any unexpected situations.

### General Travel Safety

Lake Garda is considered a safe destination, with low crime rates and a strong presence of local authorities. However, travelers should always take precautions to avoid potential inconveniences.

**Personal Safety**
- Pickpocketing Awareness: While serious crime is rare, tourist areas can attract pickpockets, particularly in crowded places like ferry terminals, markets, and bus stations. Keeping valuables secure in a crossbody bag or money belt minimizes risk.
- Avoiding Scams: Common tourist scams, such as overpriced taxis, misleading restaurant charges, or fake petitions, can occur in any major travel destination. Always confirm prices beforehand, check receipts, and avoid engaging with unsolicited offers.
- Emergency Numbers: Italy's general emergency number is **112**, which connects to police, medical assistance, and fire services.

**Road Safety**
- Driving Considerations: Roads around Lake Garda can be narrow and winding, especially on the western side. Italian drivers can be assertive, and local traffic laws require full attention. Speed limits are enforced, and fines for traffic violations can be high.
- Pedestrian Awareness: Many lakeside towns have pedestrian-friendly areas, but vehicles still operate in some sections. Paying attention when crossing roads, particularly near ferry ports, prevents accidents.

## Water Safety
➡ Swimming Guidelines: The lake is generally safe for swimming, with designated areas free of boat traffic. Checking for local safety flags and posted guidelines helps avoid strong currents or unexpected changes in water conditions.
➡ Boating Caution: Many visitors rent boats to explore the lake, but basic knowledge of boating rules is essential. Life jackets should be worn, and rental agencies provide safety briefings before departure.

## Hiking and Outdoor Safety
➡ Trail Conditions: Lake Garda's hiking trails vary in difficulty, from easy walks along the shoreline to more challenging mountain routes. Proper footwear and sufficient water supply are necessary, especially in hot weather.
➡ Wildlife Awareness: Encounters with wildlife, such as small reptiles or mountain goats, are possible in remote areas, but they are rarely a threat. Staying on marked trails helps avoid unexpected interactions.

## Nighttime Safety
➡ Well-Lit Areas: Most towns around the lake have well-lit streets and active nightlife, making them safe for evening walks. However, sticking to main roads and avoiding isolated areas is recommended.
➡ Transportation Planning: Public transport schedules vary in the evening, with some ferry and bus services ending early. Confirming the last departure times prevents being stranded in a different town.

## Health and Well-Being Considerations

Lake Garda's environment is ideal for relaxation and outdoor activities, but taking care of personal well-being ensures a pleasant visit.

### Healthcare Services

⇨ Pharmacies: Italian pharmacies (**farmacia**) are easily accessible in every town, offering medications, first aid supplies, and advice from pharmacists.

⇨ Hospitals and Clinics: Larger towns, such as Desenzano del Garda and Riva del Garda, have hospitals with emergency services. Smaller villages have medical clinics that handle minor concerns.

⇨ European Health Insurance Card (EHIC) & Travel Insurance: EU citizens can access Italian healthcare with an EHIC, though additional travel insurance is recommended for comprehensive coverage. Non-EU travelers should ensure their insurance covers medical treatment and emergencies.

### Climate and Seasonal Considerations

⇨ Summer Heat Precautions: Temperatures can rise above **30°C (86°F)** in July and August. Staying hydrated, using sunscreen, and wearing a hat help prevent heat exhaustion.

⇨ Allergy Awareness: Spring and summer bring high pollen levels, which may affect travelers with allergies. Carrying antihistamines can help ease symptoms.

⇨ Winter Conditions: The lake's mild winters are generally snow-free at lower elevations, but mountain areas can experience cold temperatures and icy trails. Packing appropriate clothing is essential for those visiting in colder months.

### Food and Water Safety

⇨ Drinking Water: Tap water around Lake Garda is safe to drink, with many public fountains available for refilling bottles. Bottled water is also widely available.

⇨ Local Cuisine Considerations: Italian food is rich in flavor, and while most travelers enjoy the cuisine without issue, those with dietary restrictions should communicate their needs clearly in restaurants. Many menus offer vegetarian, gluten-free, or dairy-free options.

## Preventing Common Illnesses

➡ Motion Sickness: Some ferry rides across the lake can be choppy, especially in windy conditions. Motion sickness tablets can help those prone to nausea.

➡ Mosquito Bites: In summer, mosquitoes can be present near the water, especially in the evenings. Using insect repellent and wearing light, long-sleeved clothing reduces the chance of bites.

With proper planning and awareness, a visit to Lake Garda is both safe and enjoyable. Italy's reliable services and friendly atmosphere make it easy for travelers to feel comfortable throughout their stay.

## Road and Transportation Safety

Getting around Lake Garda is generally straightforward, but road and transportation safety should always be a priority. The lake's varied terrain means that travel conditions can change depending on the chosen route, mode of transport, and time of year.

## Driving Considerations

➡ Road Conditions: The roads around Lake Garda vary from wide, well-paved highways to narrow, winding mountain roads. The western shore, in particular, has tight bends and tunnels carved into the cliffs, requiring extra caution.

➡ Speed Limits: The general speed limits in Italy are **50 km/h (31 mph) in towns, 90 km/h (56 mph) on rural roads, and 130 km/h (81 mph) on highways**, unless otherwise posted. Speed cameras are common, and fines for violations can be steep.

➡ Parking Challenges: Many lakeside towns have limited parking, especially during peak tourist seasons. Paid parking lots are available, but they fill up quickly. Some areas require a **disco orario**, a time-stamped parking disc available from local shops.

## Public Transportation Safety

➪ Buses: The local bus network is reliable but can be crowded, particularly in summer. It's important to keep an eye on personal belongings and ensure you board the correct route, as schedules vary between towns.

➪ Ferries: The ferry system is one of the best ways to travel between lakeside towns. While generally safe, passengers should take care when boarding, especially in rougher waters. Life jackets are available onboard, and staff members are trained for emergencies.

## Cycling and Walking

➪ Cycling Routes: Lake Garda has many scenic cycling paths, but sharing the road with cars is sometimes necessary. Wearing a helmet is advised, and using bike lights in the evening improves visibility.

➪ Pedestrian Safety: Many old town centers have cobblestone streets, which can be uneven. Comfortable, sturdy footwear helps prevent slips, especially after rain.

## Taxis and Ride-Sharing

➪ Taxis: Official taxis are safe and regulated but can be expensive, particularly for longer distances. They are usually metered, but confirming the fare before starting a trip avoids surprises.

➪ Ride-Sharing Apps: Services like Uber are not widely available in Lake Garda, so relying on traditional taxis or public transportation is often the best option.

---

## Outdoor Adventure Precautions

Lake Garda offers numerous outdoor activities, from hiking and rock climbing to watersports and cycling. Taking the right precautions ensures a safe and enjoyable experience.

## Hiking Safety

➪ Trail Selection: The trails around Lake Garda range from easy walks to steep mountain climbs. Checking the difficulty level before setting out ensures the right choice for your fitness level.

➪ Weather Awareness: Sudden weather changes can occur in mountainous areas. Carrying a light waterproof jacket and checking forecasts before starting a hike is recommended.

➪ Essential Gear: Proper hiking shoes, a map or GPS device, and sufficient water are necessary for longer trails.

## Water Activities

➪ Swimming Guidelines: While the lake is generally safe for swimming, designated swim areas should be used to avoid boat traffic. Some parts of the lake have deeper waters with sudden drop-offs.

➪ Boating and Sailing: Life jackets should always be worn, and rental operators provide safety instructions before departure. Strong winds, such as the Ora and Peler, can create challenging conditions for inexperienced sailors.

➪ Windsurfing and Kitesurfing: Lake Garda is famous for windsurfing, particularly in the northern towns of Riva del Garda and Torbole. Beginners should stick to designated learning areas, where instructors can provide guidance.

## Rock Climbing and Via Ferrata

➪ Safety Equipment: Climbing routes require proper gear, including helmets, harnesses, and sturdy climbing shoes.

➪ Supervised Routes: If unfamiliar with the area, joining a guided climbing tour provides extra safety. The via ferrata (protected climbing routes) are well-maintained but still require caution.

## Emergency Services and Contacts

Knowing how to reach emergency services ensures quick assistance in unexpected situations. Italy has a well-developed emergency response system, and services are available across Lake Garda.

## Emergency Numbers

➪ **112 – General Emergency Services:** This number connects to police, medical, and fire services.

➪ **118 – Medical Emergency:** Direct line for ambulances and urgent medical care.

⇨ **115 – Fire Department:** For fire-related emergencies, including rescue operations.
⇨ **113 – Police:** For non-urgent police assistance.
⇨ **1530 – Coast Guard:** For emergencies on the lake, including boat accidents.

**Hospitals and Clinics**
⇨ **Major Hospitals:** Larger towns, such as Desenzano del Garda and Riva del Garda, have hospitals with emergency departments.
⇨ **Local Clinics:** Smaller towns have walk-in clinics for minor medical concerns. Pharmacies (**farmacia**) provide over-the-counter medications and basic health advice.

**Lost or Stolen Items**
⇨ Police Stations: Reporting lost or stolen passports, wallets, or valuables should be done at the nearest police station (**Carabinieri or Polizia di Stato**).
⇨ Embassy Assistance: If a passport is lost, contacting your country's embassy in Italy is necessary for a replacement document.

**Roadside Assistance**
⇨ ACI (Automobile Club d'Italia): Italy's roadside assistance service can be reached at **803 116** for breakdowns and towing.
With these precautions in mind, traveling around Lake Garda becomes a smooth and worry-free experience. Being prepared for different situations ensures that any minor issues don't disrupt the trip.

# CHAPTER 2: PLANNING YOUR IDEAL TRIP

## Getting to Lake Garda

Reaching Lake Garda is straightforward, with multiple transportation options that suit different travel styles. The lake's location in northern Italy makes it well-connected to major cities like Milan, Venice, and Verona. Arriving by air, train, or car all have their advantages, depending on where you're coming from and how you prefer to travel.

### Nearest Airports and Transfer Options

For most travelers, flying is the quickest and most convenient way to reach Lake Garda. Thanks to its central location in northern Italy, the lake is well-served by several airports, each offering different advantages based on budget, route availability, and proximity to the lake's towns. Choosing the right airport can make the journey smoother, and understanding transfer options ensures an efficient trip to your final destination.

**Major Airports Serving Lake Garda**
➩ **Verona Villafranca Airport (VRN)** – This is the closest airport to Lake Garda, located roughly 15 kilometers from the

southeastern shore. It's an excellent choice for those staying in towns like Peschiera del Garda, Lazise, Bardolino, and Garda. While it primarily serves European destinations, it offers seasonal flights from other parts of the world. The airport is compact, easy to navigate, and well-connected to the lake.

➡ **Bergamo Orio al Serio Airport (BGY)** – Located about 90 kilometers from Lake Garda, Bergamo is a popular hub for budget airlines, particularly Ryanair and other low-cost carriers. It's a good option for travelers looking for affordable flights from across Europe. The airport is modern, with good facilities, and has several transportation links to reach the lake.

➡ **Milan Malpensa Airport (MXP) and Milan Linate Airport (LIN)** – These two airports are located west of Lake Garda and offer a much wider range of international flights. Malpensa, about 180 kilometers away, is Italy's second-largest airport and a major entry point for long-haul travelers from North America, Asia, and the Middle East. Linate, at 140 kilometers away, mainly serves domestic and short-haul European routes. While farther from the lake, these airports provide good onward travel connections.

➡ **Venice Marco Polo Airport (VCE)** – Roughly 150 kilometers east of Lake Garda, this airport is a great option for those combining a trip to the lake with Venice. It offers international flights and is well-connected by road and rail to northern Italy.

### Transfer Options from the Airports

Once you land, there are several ways to get to Lake Garda, each with its own balance of convenience, speed, and cost.

### Private Transfers

For the fastest and most comfortable journey, private transfers are available from all major airports. Companies offer door-to-door service, ensuring a smooth trip without the hassle of public transport. Prices vary based on the distance, with Verona transfers being the most affordable.

➡ Verona to Lake Garda: Approx. €50–€100, 20–40 minutes
➡ Bergamo to Lake Garda: Approx. €120–€180, 1.5–2 hours

➡ Milan to Lake Garda: Approx. €150–€250, 2–3 hours
➡ Venice to Lake Garda: Approx. €130–€200, 2–2.5 hours

**Car Rentals**

Renting a car is a great option for those wanting flexibility. All major airports have rental agencies offering vehicles suited for different budgets. The roads to Lake Garda are well-maintained, and driving provides the freedom to explore the region at your own pace.

➡ Tolls: Italian highways require toll payments, which can be made in cash, by card, or using a prepaid Telepass.
➡ Parking: Most towns have designated parking areas, with paid options near the lake and free spaces slightly farther out.
➡ Driving Time: From Verona, the drive is under 30 minutes. From Milan or Venice, expect a journey of around 2 hours.

**Buses and Trains**

For those relying on public transport, buses and trains offer a cost-effective way to reach the lake.

➡ Verona Airport to Lake Garda: Direct shuttle buses run from Verona Airport to Peschiera del Garda and Desenzano. From there, local buses serve other lakeside towns.
➡ Bergamo Airport: Buses connect the airport to Bergamo's main train station, where travelers can take a train to Desenzano or Peschiera.
➡ Milan and Venice Airports: The best option is taking a train from Milan or Venice to one of Lake Garda's two main train stations (Desenzano del Garda or Peschiera del Garda).

## Train Routes and Stations

Italy's rail network makes reaching Lake Garda by train an easy and scenic option. Trains provide a comfortable and efficient way to travel, especially for those arriving from other Italian cities or European destinations.

## Main Train Stations Serving Lake Garda

Unlike some of Italy's other lakes, Lake Garda doesn't have a train line running directly along its shores. However, two key railway stations serve the southern part of the lake, offering good connections to major cities.

- **Desenzano del Garda-Sirmione Station** – Located on the southwestern side of the lake, Desenzano's station is a primary hub for travelers heading to Sirmione, Desenzano, and nearby towns. It's on the Milan-Venice railway line, making it an ideal stop for those coming from either city. The station has taxis, bus services, and a ferry terminal nearby, making onward travel easy.
- **Peschiera del Garda Station** – Located southeast of the lake, this station is another key entry point, especially for those heading to towns like Lazise, Bardolino, or Garda. Like Desenzano, it sits on the Milan-Venice line and offers frequent regional and high-speed trains.

### Train Routes to Lake Garda

- **From Milan:** High-speed and regional trains run frequently from Milano Centrale to Desenzano del Garda and Peschiera del Garda. The journey takes about one hour, making it a quick and convenient option.
- **From Venice:** Direct trains from Venezia Santa Lucia to Desenzano or Peschiera take around 90 minutes. Some trains may require a change in Verona.
- **From Florence:** Travelers can take a high-speed train from Firenze Santa Maria Novella to Verona, then transfer to a regional train for the final leg to Lake Garda. The total journey takes about 3 hours.
- **From Rome:** Direct high-speed trains connect Rome to Verona in about 3 hours, followed by a short regional train ride to the lake.

## Booking Train Tickets

Train tickets can be booked online via **Trenitalia** or **Italo**, the two major railway operators in Italy. Tickets are also available at station kiosks and ticket counters.

➡ Regional Trains: These are cheaper and do not require seat reservations. They stop at more stations, making them ideal for budget travelers.

➡ High-Speed Trains: These require seat reservations and offer a faster, more comfortable ride with onboard services like Wi-Fi and refreshments.

## Getting from the Train Station to the Lake

Once at Desenzano or Peschiera stations, travelers have several options to reach their final destination.

➡ Taxis: Readily available outside the stations, taxis are the fastest but most expensive option.

➡ Buses: Local buses connect the stations to other lakeside towns, with frequent services during peak season.

➡ Ferries: Desenzano has a ferry terminal within walking distance from the train station, allowing travelers to continue their journey by boat.

For those planning to stay on the northern side of the lake (Riva del Garda, Malcesine, Limone), reaching these areas by train requires additional connections via bus or ferry. While this takes longer, it offers a scenic route through the region.

## Driving to Lake Garda: Road Trip Tips

Driving to Lake Garda is one of the best ways to experience northern Italy at your own pace. The region is well-connected by highways, and the scenic roads around the lake make for a rewarding journey. Whether you're arriving from within Italy or a neighboring country, planning ahead ensures a smooth and enjoyable trip.

## Best Routes to Lake Garda

The route to Lake Garda will depend on your starting point, but most travelers use Italy's **Autostrada** (highway) system to reach the lake efficiently.

⇨ From Milan – The A4 Autostrada (Milan-Venice) is the most direct route. Exit at Desenzano del Garda, Sirmione, or Peschiera del Garda for access to the southern towns.

⇨ From Venice – The same A4 Autostrada connects Venice to Lake Garda. The drive takes about 1.5 hours, with Peschiera del Garda being the most convenient exit.

⇨ From Verona – The A22 Autostrada (Brenner-Modena) is the best choice for those heading to the northern towns like Riva del Garda, Limone, or Malcesine. If heading to the southern shore, take the A4 Autostrada instead.

⇨ From Austria/Germany – Travelers coming from the north will use the A22 Autostrada via the Brenner Pass. This scenic Alpine route leads directly to Rovereto, the nearest major exit for northern Lake Garda.

⇨ From Florence or Rome – The A1 Autostrada connects central and southern Italy to the north. At Modena, switch to the A22 Autostrada to reach the lake.

## Driving Conditions and Road Etiquette

Driving in Italy is generally straightforward, but understanding local road rules and conditions helps ensure a stress-free trip.

⇨ Toll Roads – Major highways (Autostrade) are toll roads. Tolls can be paid in cash, by card, or via Telepass (electronic toll payment). Expect to pay around **€10–€15** for a trip from Milan or Venice to Lake Garda.

⇨ Speed Limits – The limits vary by road type:
  ❖ Highways: **130 km/h** (or **110 km/h** in rain)
  ❖ Main roads: **90 km/h**
  ❖ Urban areas: **50 km/h**

⇨ Driving Style – Italian drivers can be assertive. Stay in the right lane unless overtaking, use turn signals clearly, and be cautious at roundabouts.

➡ Fuel Stations – Gas stations are widely available. Self-service pumps are usually cheaper, and some stations close at night, though automated pumps are available 24/7.

## Scenic Drives Around Lake Garda

Once you reach the lake, the **Gardesana** road (SR249) offers a breathtaking drive along the shoreline.

➡ Southern Route (Desenzano to Peschiera) – A relatively easy drive, passing through Sirmione and Lazise, with plenty of spots to stop for lakeside views.

➡ Western Route (Salò to Riva del Garda) – This road hugs the cliffs and offers spectacular scenery, but it can be narrow and winding, requiring careful driving.

➡ Eastern Route (Peschiera to Malcesine) – A smooth, well-maintained road passing through Bardolino, Garda, and Torri del Benaco, with frequent viewpoints.

➡ Northern Route (Riva del Garda to Limone) – A dramatic, winding stretch with tunnels carved into the cliffs and stunning lake views.

## Parking and ZTL Zones

Most towns around Lake Garda have **ZTL (Zona a Traffico Limitato)** areas, where only authorized vehicles can enter. These are usually in historic centers, and driving into them without permission can result in a fine.

➡ Parking Lots – Paid parking is available near town centers, with rates around €1–€2 per hour. Free parking is available farther from the lake.

➡ Blue Lines – Indicate paid parking areas.

➡ White Lines – Free parking (where allowed).

➡ Yellow Lines – Reserved for residents or special permits.

## Final Tips for a Smooth Road Trip

➡ Have cash and a card for tolls, as some booths don't accept foreign credit cards.

➡ Keep an eye on fuel levels, especially when driving in rural areas.

➡ Use Google Maps or Waze for real-time traffic updates, as summer congestion is common.

➡ If renting a car, request an automatic transmission in advance, as most rentals in Italy are manual.

➡ Be patient in high-traffic areas, particularly on weekends and in peak summer months.

Driving around Lake Garda is a rewarding experience, allowing you to stop at scenic viewpoints, small villages, and hidden beaches along the way.

# Crafting the Perfect Itinerary

Planning your time at Lake Garda depends on how long you have and what kind of experience you're looking for. The lake offers everything from historic towns and scenic drives to outdoor adventures and wine tasting. A weekend trip allows for a highlights tour, while a weeklong stay gives you time to explore different areas in depth.

## Weekend Escape Recommendations

A short visit to Lake Garda means prioritizing the must-see spots and balancing sightseeing with relaxation. With just two or three days, focusing on the southern or northern part of the lake makes the most sense, as trying to cover too much ground can feel rushed.

### Day 1: Southern Lake Garda – History, Lakeside Strolls, and Wine

#### 🖥 Morning: Arrival and Sirmione

Arriving at Lake Garda early allows you to make the most of the day. A good starting point is Sirmione, one of the most scenic towns on the lake. The medieval Scaliger Castle, with its striking location on the water, sets the tone for the visit. After exploring the fortress, take a walk through Sirmione's narrow streets, stopping for a coffee or gelato.

## ⏱ Midday: Relaxation at the Thermal Baths or a Boat Tour

Sirmione is known for its thermal waters, so consider unwinding at Aquaria Thermal Spa, which overlooks the lake. If you prefer to stay active, taking a boat tour around the peninsula provides a different perspective of the town and a close-up view of Grotte di Catullo, the ruins of an ancient Roman villa.

## Afternoon: Wine Tasting in Lugana

A short drive south leads to the Lugana wine region, where local wineries offer tastings of their crisp white wines. Some of the best wineries include Ca' dei Frati and Zenato, both known for high-quality Lugana wines.

## Evening: Dinner in Desenzano del Garda

Ending the day in Desenzano del Garda provides a lively atmosphere with plenty of lakeside restaurants. Trattorias here serve fresh lake fish and homemade pasta, making it a great place to experience regional cuisine.

## Day 2: Northern Lake Garda – Mountains, Adventure, and Scenic Views

## Morning: Riva del Garda and the Ponale Trail

Head to the northern part of the lake, where the landscapes become more mountainous. Riva del Garda is an ideal base for outdoor activities. The Ponale Trail, a scenic hiking and cycling path carved into the cliffs, offers panoramic views over the lake and takes about two hours to complete round-trip.

## ⏱ Midday: Lunch in Limone sul Garda

A short drive or ferry ride from Riva, Limone sul Garda is famous for its lemon groves and charming streets. A lakeside restaurant is the perfect place to enjoy fresh seafood or a plate of pasta with local olive oil.

## Afternoon: Malcesine and Monte Baldo

Across the lake from Limone, Malcesine is another must-visit town. After strolling through its medieval center and visiting Scaliger Castle, take the Monte Baldo cable car up to breathtaking viewpoints. The top offers hiking trails and, in cooler months, the chance to see snow-capped peaks.

### 🖥 Morning:Evening: Sunset and Departure

Before leaving, find a quiet lakeside spot to enjoy the sunset. If you're staying the night, Malcesine or Riva del Garda both have excellent restaurants for a final dinner on the lake.

## One-Week Travel Plans

A full week at Lake Garda allows time to experience different regions, mix relaxation with activities, and enjoy local food and wine.

### Day 1: Arrival and Exploring the Southern Shore

⇨ Start in Sirmione, visiting Scaliger Castle and Grotte di Catullo.

⇨ Relax at Aquaria Thermal Spa or take a short boat trip.

⇨ Drive to Desenzano del Garda for dinner and an evening walk along the promenade.

### Day 2: Cultural Stops and Wine Tasting

⇨ Visit Salò, a town known for its elegant streets and history.

⇨ Explore Gardone Riviera, home to Il Vittoriale degli Italiani, the former estate of poet Gabriele D'Annunzio.

⇨ In the afternoon, stop at a Valtenesi winery for a tasting of rosé and red wines.

⇨ Stay overnight in Salò or Gardone Riviera.

### Day 3: Adventure and the Western Cliffs

⇨ Drive north along the Gardesana Occidentale, one of the most scenic roads in Italy.

⇨ Stop at Limone sul Garda, known for its lemon groves and picturesque harbor.

⇨ Continue to Riva del Garda for lunch.

⇨ Spend the afternoon hiking the Ponale Trail or visiting Cascata del Varone, a waterfall just outside town.

⇨ Stay in Riva del Garda for the night.

### Day 4: Northern Lake and Monte Baldo

⇨ Take the Monte Baldo cable car from Malcesine in the morning.

⇨ Explore the medieval streets of Malcesine, including Scaliger Castle.

⇨ Spend the afternoon at a lakeside beach or take a ferry across to Limone sul Garda.

⇨ Enjoy a relaxed dinner with a view.

**Day 5: The Eastern Shore and Bardolino Wine Country**

⇨ Visit Torri del Benaco, a quiet lakeside town with a small but charming historic center.

⇨ Stop at Punta San Vigilio, a peaceful peninsula with a famous waterfront café.

⇨ In the afternoon, head inland to Bardolino and visit wineries specializing in Bardolino red and Chiaretto rosé wines.

⇨ Stay in Bardolino or Lazise for the night.

**Day 6: Relaxation and Leisure**

⇨ Spend the morning at Jamaica Beach in Sirmione, one of the lake's most scenic swimming spots.

⇨ Take a boat tour of the lake, stopping at lesser-visited villages.

⇨ Visit Lazise, a small town with well-preserved medieval walls and a lively lakefront.

⇨ Have a final evening meal in a lakeside restaurant.

**Day 7: A Final Morning in Lake Garda**

⇨ If time allows, enjoy a relaxed breakfast by the lake.

⇨ Visit a local market to pick up regional products before departure.

A week at Lake Garda offers a balance of sightseeing, relaxation, and outdoor activities, ensuring a complete experience of Italy's largest lake.

# Budget and Money-Saving Advice

A trip to Lake Garda can be tailored to fit different budgets, from affordable stays to luxury experiences. Planning ahead and knowing where to spend or save makes all the difference. Understanding typical costs and finding ways to reduce expenses ensures a rewarding trip without unnecessary spending.

## Estimated Costs for Different Budgets

Costs vary depending on travel style, season, and preferences. Below is a breakdown of daily expenses for budget, mid-range, and luxury travelers.

**Budget Traveler (€50–€100 per day per person)**
- ⇨ Accommodation: €20–€50 per night (hostels, guesthouses, budget hotels, or camping sites)
- ⇨ Food: €5–€10 for breakfast, €10–€15 for lunch, €15 for dinner (self-catering, casual eateries, or pizzerias)
- ⇨ Transport: €5–€15 (public buses, regional trains, or bike rentals)
- ⇨ Attractions: €10–€20 (some museums and historical sites charge small entrance fees, outdoor activities are often free)

For budget travelers, choosing guesthouses or camping sites, eating at bakeries or local trattorias, and relying on public transport helps keep costs low.

**Mid-Range Traveler (€100–€250 per day per person)**
- ⇨ Accommodation: €80–€150 per night (mid-range hotels or lakeview B&Bs)
- ⇨ Food: €10–€20 for breakfast, €20–€30 for lunch, €30–€50 for dinner (restaurants, wine tastings, and lakeside dining)
- ⇨ Transport: €10–€30 (car rental or ferry rides)
- ⇨ Attractions: €20–€50 (cable car rides, boat tours, and guided experiences)

Mid-range travelers enjoy a mix of comfort and experience. Opting for locally owned hotels, dining at family-run restaurants, and using ferries to explore different towns balances cost and quality.

**Luxury Traveler (€250+ per day per person)**
- ⇨ Accommodation: €250+ per night (high-end lakefront hotels, resorts, or private villas)
- ⇨ Food: €20–€40 for breakfast, €40–€80 for lunch, €80+ for dinner (fine dining, Michelin-star restaurants, and private tastings)
- ⇨ Transport: €50–€150 (private transfers, rental cars, or yacht rentals)
- ⇨ Attractions: €50–€200+ (exclusive tours, private boat charters, spa treatments, and wine experiences)

For a luxury experience, staying in a lakefront suite, booking private tours, and dining at top restaurants provide a high level of comfort and exclusivity.

## Cost-Effective Travel Tips

Lake Garda offers ways to save money without compromising the experience. Small adjustments make a significant impact on the overall budget.

**1. Visit in the Shoulder Seasons:** Traveling in late spring or early autumn means lower hotel prices, fewer crowds, and comfortable weather. July and August are the most expensive months, with higher accommodation rates and packed attractions.

**2. Stay in Smaller Towns:** While Sirmione and Riva del Garda are popular, nearby towns such as Peschiera del Garda, Torri del Benaco, and Salò offer more affordable lodging. Guesthouses and family-run B&Bs often provide better value than large hotels.

**3. Use Public Transport:** Buses and regional trains connect major towns and cost significantly less than rental cars. Ferries are a scenic and budget-friendly way to move between towns, especially with a day pass.

**4. Choose Free and Low-Cost Attractions:** Many of Lake Garda's highlights don't require an entrance fee. Strolling through medieval villages, hiking scenic trails, and swimming in the lake are all free. Some historical sites, like castles and museums, have low-cost entry tickets.

**5. Eat Like a Local:** Instead of dining at tourist-heavy spots, look for trattorias and agriturismos (farmhouse restaurants) that serve authentic meals at fair prices. Ordering a "menu del giorno" (daily set menu) often includes multiple courses at a lower cost.

**6. Buy Groceries for Some Meals:** Local markets and supermarkets offer fresh ingredients at a fraction of restaurant prices. Picking up bread, cheese, and fruit for a picnic lunch can save money while offering a relaxed meal by the lake.

**7. Look for Accommodation Deals:** Booking directly with hotels or using rental platforms often leads to better rates than third-party booking sites. Many places offer discounts for longer stays or off-season reservations.

**8. Plan Paid Experiences Wisely:** Instead of multiple expensive activities, choose one or two highlights. A boat rental, cable car ride, or wine tour can be the centerpiece of the trip while balancing free experiences throughout the day.

**9. Take Advantage of City Cards and Passes:** Some towns offer discount cards that provide access to public transport and attractions at a reduced rate. Checking local tourism offices for special deals can lead to additional savings.

**10. Travel with a Group:** Costs for accommodation, car rentals, and even meals are often lower when split among friends or family. Many hotels and rental apartments offer discounts for group bookings.

# CHAPTER 3: EXPLORING SIRMIONE

Sirmione is one of the most captivating towns on Lake Garda, set on a narrow peninsula that stretches into the southern waters of Italy's largest lake. With its charming streets, historic landmarks, and thermal springs, Sirmione draws visitors seeking both relaxation and a deep connection to its storied past. The town's roots run deep, going back thousands of years, and every cobbled pathway seems to whisper tales of emperors, poets, and fierce battles.

## Historical Significance

Sirmione's past is layered with centuries of human settlement, military strategy, and cultural flourishing. From Roman occupation to medieval conflicts, the town has long held strategic and symbolic importance. This section details the key historical moments that shaped Sirmione into the treasured destination it is today.

### Ancient Roots of Sirmione

Sirmione's history stretches back thousands of years, long before it became the elegant lakeside retreat it is today. The town's unique geographical position—a narrow peninsula extending into Lake Garda—made it an ideal settlement for early inhabitants. Over time, it evolved from a simple lakeside dwelling into a thriving center of Roman luxury, with grand villas, sophisticated infrastructure, and mineral-rich thermal springs that still define its character.

## Prehistoric Settlements and Early Inhabitants

The earliest evidence of human presence around Lake Garda dates back to the Bronze Age, approximately 2000 BCE. Archaeological discoveries, including ancient pile dwellings (stilt houses), suggest that prehistoric communities lived in and around Sirmione's peninsula, benefiting from the lake's abundant resources. These stilt houses, remnants of which have been found in the surrounding region, indicate that early inhabitants adapted to life on the water, possibly to avoid flooding or for protection against wild animals and rival tribes.

The lake provided fish, while the fertile land supported agriculture. Over time, these small settlements grew into more organized communities, developing trade with neighboring regions. By the late Bronze Age, Sirmione and other lakeside settlements had established networks that connected them to other parts of northern Italy. Artifacts found in the area, such as tools, pottery, and weapons, suggest a community that thrived on fishing, farming, and trade.

## The Arrival of the Romans

By the 1st century BCE, the Romans had expanded their influence across northern Italy, and Sirmione became part of their vast empire. Recognizing the peninsula's strategic and geographical advantages, the Romans developed it into a hub of commerce, defense, and leisure. The town's location provided natural protection, making it a valuable stronghold, while its scenic setting and access to thermal waters made it a desirable retreat for the wealthy elite.

Roman engineers introduced significant infrastructure improvements, including roads, fortifications, and aqueducts. Sirmione was integrated into the **Via Gallica**, a major Roman road that connected the region to Verona, Brescia, and Milan. This network allowed for the movement of goods, soldiers, and travelers, ensuring Sirmione remained an active part of the empire's northern territories.

## Grotte di Catullo: The Grandeur of Roman Villas

Perhaps the most enduring testament to Sirmione's Roman legacy is the Grotte di Catullo, the remains of a vast Roman villa dating back to the 1st century CE. Despite its name—"Grotte" meaning caves—the site is not a natural cave but rather the ruins of an opulent estate that once stood atop the peninsula's highest point.

This villa, likely built by a wealthy Roman family, was a sprawling complex of grand halls, gardens, terraces, and bathing areas, covering nearly two hectares. Though time has eroded much of its structure, the remnants reveal impressive architectural feats. Visitors today can still see the outlines of large columns, mosaic floors, and sections of hypocaust heating systems, which were used to warm the villa's baths. The villa is often associated with the poet Gaius Valerius Catullus, who lived during the late Roman Republic (circa 84–54 BCE). Catullus wrote passionately about Sirmione, referring to it as a place of personal joy and retreat. While there is no definitive proof that he owned this particular villa, his poetry immortalized Sirmione as a refuge of beauty and tranquility.

**"O Sirmio, jewel of peninsulas and islands, whatever in shining waters Neptune carries..."**

These words reflect the deep admiration Romans held for this enchanting location. The association with Catullus further reinforced Sirmione's reputation as a place of inspiration for poets, intellectuals, and statesmen.

## Thermal Springs and Roman Bathing Culture

One of Sirmione's most remarkable natural features is its thermal springs, which emerge from the depths of Lake Garda. Rich in minerals such as sulfur, bromine, and iodine, these waters were believed to have therapeutic properties. The Romans, who highly valued public bathing as both a social and medicinal activity, capitalized on this resource by constructing elaborate thermal baths.

These bathing complexes were not only places for relaxation but also centers for social interaction, where political discussions, business dealings, and philosophical debates took place. The thermal baths at Sirmione likely attracted Roman aristocrats seeking rejuvenation, much as they do today.

**Religious and Cultural Influence in the Roman Period**
As Sirmione grew in prominence, so too did its cultural and religious significance. Roman influence brought the worship of classical deities, and it is believed that temples or shrines dedicated to gods such as Neptune, Venus, or Apollo may have existed in the area.

The presence of Roman villas suggests that Sirmione was home to members of the elite who participated in the intellectual and artistic movements of the time. The region likely hosted poets, philosophers, and politicians who sought refuge from the demands of urban life.

**The Decline of Roman Sirmione**
By the 4th and 5th centuries CE, the Roman Empire was in decline, and Sirmione's fortunes began to change. The once-thriving villas and bathhouses saw reduced use as political instability spread across Italy. With the fall of the Western Roman Empire in 476 CE, Sirmione entered a new era marked by uncertainty.
As waves of barbarian invasions swept through northern Italy, Sirmione's strategic position made it a contested site. The defensive advantages that once made it a haven for the elite now made it an attractive target for various factions, including the Lombards, who would later establish their own rule in the area.
Despite the empire's collapse, the legacy of Roman Sirmione endured. The ruins of the Grotte di Catullo stood as a reminder of the town's former grandeur, and the thermal springs continued to be valued for their healing properties. The infrastructure left behind by Roman engineers—particularly the road systems—ensured that Sirmione remained connected to the wider region, even as new rulers took control.

**Legacy of Sirmione's Ancient Roots**
Sirmione's transformation from a prehistoric settlement to a Roman retreat set the stage for its continued importance through the medieval and modern eras. The remnants of its Roman past remain some of the most significant archaeological sites in northern Italy, drawing historians, scholars, and travelers eager to walk in the footsteps of those who once lived here.

The Grotte di Catullo, the legacy of Catullus' poetry, and the enduring appeal of Sirmione's thermal waters all highlight the deep historical roots that continue to shape the town's identity. Even today, visitors strolling through the ruins or gazing across the lake from the ancient villa's terraces can sense the grandeur that once defined this remarkable corner of Lake Garda.

## Major Historical Events

Sirmione's long and complex history has been shaped by a series of pivotal events, from ancient times through the medieval period and into the modern era. Over the centuries, it has served as a Roman retreat, a military stronghold, a refuge for persecuted communities, and a prized possession of warring factions. Each chapter in its history has left behind tangible traces, influencing the town's character and significance within the Lake Garda region.

### Roman Rule and the Growth of Sirmione (1st Century BCE – 5th Century CE)

Sirmione first gained prominence under the Romans, who saw its strategic and geographical advantages. With the construction of **Via Gallica**, the town became well-connected to major Roman cities like Verona, Brescia, and Milan. This period saw the development of infrastructure, including villas, bathhouses, and defensive structures. The **Grotte di Catullo**, an expansive Roman villa, was built around the 1st century CE, serving as a luxurious retreat for the elite.

The decline of the Roman Empire in the 4th and 5th centuries brought instability to Sirmione. With the Western Roman Empire's fall in 476 CE, the region saw successive invasions by Germanic tribes, including the Goths and later the Lombards. These invasions disrupted life in Sirmione, leading to the gradual abandonment of Roman villas and the repurposing of structures for defense.

### The Lombard Era and the Fortification of Sirmione (6th–8th Century)

During the early medieval period, the Lombards, a Germanic people who ruled much of Italy from 568 to 774 CE, took control of Sirmione. Recognizing its defensive potential, they transformed the town into a fortified settlement. Archaeological evidence suggests the presence of defensive walls and military outposts during this time.

One of the most significant figures of this era was **Queen Ansa**, wife of the Lombard King Desiderius. Under her influence, Sirmione became an important center for religious and political activity. The town's stronghold provided refuge for those loyal to the Lombard cause, especially during Charlemagne's campaign to overthrow the Lombard Kingdom in 774 CE. When Charlemagne's forces eventually conquered the Lombards, Sirmione fell under the rule of the **Carolingian Empire**, marking a new chapter in its history.

### The Rise of the Scaliger Castle (13th Century)

During the 13th century, northern Italy was divided among powerful city-states and noble families. Sirmione became a focal point of these territorial struggles. In 1277, the **Scaliger family**, rulers of Verona, took control of the town and commissioned the construction of **Rocca Scaligera**, the iconic castle that still dominates Sirmione's skyline today.

The castle was built as both a defensive fortress and a military outpost. Surrounded by water, its design included fortified walls, drawbridges, and watchtowers, making it nearly impenetrable. This period saw Sirmione's transformation from a Roman retreat to a strategically vital military site.

### The Cathar Persecution and Sirmione's Role (13th Century)

One of the most dramatic and tragic events in Sirmione's history occurred in the late 13th century when the town became a refuge for the Cathars, a Christian sect persecuted by the Catholic Church for their beliefs. The Cathars, considered heretics, sought shelter in Sirmione's fortified walls, where they lived in relative peace for some time.

However, in 1276, troops under the command of the **Scaliger ruler Alberto della Scala** besieged Sirmione, capturing the Cathar community. Hundreds of Cathars were arrested and later executed in the **Arena di Verona**, marking one of the most brutal episodes of religious persecution in medieval Italy. This event cemented

Sirmione's place in the religious conflicts that shaped Europe during the Middle Ages.

**Venetian Rule and the Renaissance Influence (15th–18th Century)**
By the early 15th century, Sirmione had come under the control of the **Republic of Venice**. The Venetian rulers maintained the fortress and continued to use Sirmione as a strategic outpost. Under their administration, trade flourished, and the town's role as a defensive site remained crucial, especially during conflicts with neighboring city-states.
Venetian influence extended beyond military affairs; it also shaped Sirmione's cultural and architectural development. Many of the town's existing structures, including churches and civic buildings, were either built or modified during this period. Trade connections between Sirmione and Venice ensured economic stability, allowing the town to develop a more refined character, balancing its military function with its role as a commercial and residential hub.

**Napoleonic Wars and Austrian Occupation (18th–19th Century)**
The late 18th and early 19th centuries were turbulent for Sirmione, as northern Italy became a battleground for European powers. With the rise of **Napoleon Bonaparte**, French forces took control of the region, leading to the decline of Venetian rule. Sirmione, like much of Lombardy, became part of the **Napoleonic Kingdom of Italy (1805–1814)** before being absorbed into the Austrian Empire after Napoleon's defeat.
Under Austrian rule, Sirmione remained strategically important but experienced economic stagnation. The Austrians strengthened military presence in the region, fearing insurrections and foreign invasions. However, by the mid-19th century, Italian nationalism was on the rise, and Sirmione found itself caught in the larger movement toward Italian unification.

**Italian Unification and the Modern Era (19th–20th Century)**
In 1861, Italy was officially unified, and Sirmione became part of the newly established **Kingdom of Italy**. This transition marked the

beginning of a new era, as the town gradually shifted from a military stronghold to a destination known for its cultural and natural appeal.

By the late 19th and early 20th centuries, Sirmione's thermal springs, long known for their healing properties, attracted renewed interest. The construction of modern thermal bath facilities led to a revival in tourism, drawing visitors from across Italy and beyond.

During World War II, Sirmione, like much of northern Italy, witnessed the impact of conflict. German forces occupied the region, and the town saw military activity as part of the broader struggle between Axis and Allied powers. After the war, Sirmione's focus shifted toward economic recovery and tourism development, setting the stage for its modern identity as a lakeside retreat.

### Sirmione in the 21st Century

Today, Sirmione stands as a place where history and modernity coexist. The legacy of its major historical events—Roman grandeur, medieval conflicts, Venetian rule, and the struggles for Italian unification—can still be seen in its streets, buildings, and archaeological sites.

While it remains a tourist destination, Sirmione's historical significance is far more than just an attraction. The events that shaped this town continue to define its identity, making it one of the most historically rich locations along the shores of **Lake Garda**.

## Must-See Attractions

Sirmione is packed with historical landmarks, stunning landscapes, and cultural treasures that have made it one of the most compelling destinations along Lake Garda. Among its many attractions, two stand out for their historical significance and architectural beauty: Scaliger Castle, a perfectly preserved medieval fortress, and the Grottoes of Catullus, the remains of a grand Roman villa that offers insight into the town's ancient past. These sites are not just remnants of history— they are windows into the lives of those who shaped Sirmione over the centuries.

## Scaliger Castle: A Medieval Gem

🏠 **Address:** Piazza Castello, 34, 25019 Sirmione BS, Italy

📍 **GPS Coordinates:** 45.4953° N, 10.6091° E

Standing at the entrance of Sirmione's historic center, Scaliger Castle (Rocca Scaligera) is impossible to miss. Its towering stone walls, imposing battlements, and fortified towers create a striking introduction to the town, setting the stage for the history and charm that lie beyond. Built in the 13th century by the Scaliger family, rulers of Verona, the castle served as both a military fortress and a strategic gateway to the peninsula. Today, it is one of the best-preserved castles in Italy and a remarkable example of medieval fortification.

The first thing that stands out about Scaliger Castle is its location. Surrounded by water on all sides, it appears almost like a floating stronghold, an illusion enhanced by its well-preserved moat. The castle's design was intentionally defensive, with high walls, narrow windows for archers, and a drawbridge that originally restricted access to the town. Its construction was not just about protection, though—it was also a clear message of power from the Scaliger rulers, reinforcing their dominance over Sirmione and its valuable trade routes.

One of the best ways to experience the castle is by climbing to the top of the main tower. The 146 steps to the highest point may be a workout, but the effort is rewarded with sweeping views over Lake Garda, the red-tiled rooftops of Sirmione, and the surrounding hills. From this vantage point, it is easy to see why the Scaligers chose this location—it provided a natural defense while allowing them to oversee movements on the lake.

Inside the castle walls, the courtyard and ramparts offer a closer look at medieval military architecture. The thick stone walls, wooden walkways, and lookout points all speak to a time when the threat of attack was real, and strategic defense was essential. While the interior of the castle is relatively sparse today, with only a few historical displays, the structure itself is the main attraction. Walking along the walls and peering through the arrow slits, it is easy to imagine the castle's guards keeping watch for approaching enemies.

The castle also has a unique feature that sets it apart from many other medieval fortresses—a fortified harbor. This enclosed docking area was crucial for the Scaligers, allowing them to control trade and transport across Lake Garda. Even today, the remnants of this harbor provide a fascinating look at how the castle functioned as a military base and administrative center.

Over the centuries, Scaliger Castle has stood as a silent witness to Sirmione's changing fortunes. From its time as a defensive stronghold to its later use as a Venetian military outpost and, eventually, as a historical monument, the castle has remained at the heart of the town. Visiting today, it is not just a step back into the Middle Ages but a chance to experience the enduring presence of Sirmione's past.

**How to Get There:**

Scaliger Castle is located at the entrance of Sirmione's historic center. If you are arriving by car, parking is available at Parcheggio Monte Baldo, which is about a 10-minute walk from the castle. From there, you can walk through the charming narrow streets leading to the fortress.

For those using public transport, buses from Desenzano del Garda or Peschiera del Garda frequently stop at Sirmione's main bus station, just a short walk from the castle. Alternatively, ferries from towns around Lake Garda, such as Bardolino, Lazise, and Malcesine, dock at Sirmione's port, just a few minutes away on foot.

## The Grottoes of Catullus: Roman Ruins with a View

🏠 **Address:** Piazzale Orti Manara, 4, 25019 Sirmione BS, Italy

📍 **GPS Coordinates:** 45.5005° N, 10.6064° E

At the very tip of the Sirmione peninsula lies one of the most important Roman archaeological sites in northern Italy—the Grotte di Catullo. Despite the name, these ruins are not actual grottoes but the remains of a vast Roman villa that once belonged to a wealthy noble family. The site earned its misleading name in the Renaissance period, when travelers mistakenly believed the collapsed structures resembled caves. What remains today is a sprawling complex of stone walls, archways, and foundations that offer a glimpse into the grandeur of Roman luxury.

The villa is traditionally associated with Gaius Valerius Catullus, a Roman poet who lived in the 1st century BCE. While there is no definitive proof that he resided here, Catullus did write about his family's estate on Lake Garda, leading many historians to connect him to this impressive site. Regardless of its exact ownership, the villa was undoubtedly a lavish retreat, built to take advantage of Sirmione's scenic beauty and natural hot springs.

Walking through the ruins, it is clear that this was no ordinary residence. Covering nearly two hectares, the villa featured expansive terraces, grand halls, and private bathhouses—all designed to accommodate the wealthy elite of Roman society. The structure's layout suggests a careful balance between practicality and luxury, with areas dedicated to social gatherings, relaxation, and daily living. The use of large windows and open spaces also indicates an appreciation for the surrounding landscape, reinforcing the idea that the villa was a retreat meant for pleasure and leisure.

One of the most striking features of the site is the **cryptoporticus**, a series of covered passageways that likely served as shaded walkways for the villa's residents. These subterranean corridors provided a cool escape from the summer heat, demonstrating the Romans' architectural ingenuity. Another highlight is the **large central courtyard**, which would have been lined with columns and decorative fountains, creating an elegant outdoor space for dining and entertainment.

Beyond the architectural remains, the museum on-site houses artifacts discovered during excavations, including pottery, mosaics, and sculptures. These relics help to piece together the daily lives of those who once lived here, offering a tangible connection to the past. Some of the most remarkable finds include fragments of frescoes that once adorned the villa's walls, providing hints of the artistry and craftsmanship that defined Roman high society.

Standing among the ruins today, it is easy to sense the passage of time. The same landscape that drew the Romans to Sirmione still stretches out in front of visitors—the blue expanse of Lake Garda, the distant mountains, and the gentle lapping of waves against the shore. It is a setting that has captivated people for centuries, from ancient poets to modern travelers.

The Grottoes of Catullus are more than just a collection of ancient stones; they are a testament to Sirmione's deep historical roots. The villa's ruins, the stories they hold, and the breathtaking setting make this site one of the most fascinating places to visit in the region.

**How to Get There:**
The Grottoes of Catullus are located at the far end of the Sirmione peninsula. If you are coming from the historic center, you can walk along Via S. Pietro in Mavino, a scenic route that takes about 15–20 minutes on foot. Along the way, you will pass olive groves and charming old buildings before reaching the entrance to the archaeological park.

For those who prefer not to walk, a tourist shuttle train runs from Sirmione's main square (Piazza Carducci) to the site during peak season. If you are traveling by ferry, Sirmione's port is about a 20-minute walk from the ruins.

# Experiencing Local Culture

Sirmione is more than just a historic town with breathtaking scenery—it is a place where culture comes to life through its traditions, markets, and cuisine. From the bustling energy of local markets to the flavors of authentic dishes, the town offers a taste of both past and present. Visiting during a lively festival or enjoying a quiet meal in a family-run trattoria always offers an opportunity to experience the rhythms of daily life in this lakeside gem.

## Traditional Markets and Seasonal Events

Markets have long been a central part of life in Sirmione, just as they have been in towns across Italy. They offer a direct connection to the region's agricultural roots and artisanal traditions, providing visitors with a chance to see and sample local specialties. One of the best ways to experience Sirmione like a local is to visit the weekly market, where vendors set up stalls filled with fresh produce, cheeses, cured meats, and handcrafted goods.

The **Sirmione Weekly Market** takes place every **Monday morning** at **Piazza Mercato** in Colombare, just outside the historic center. Here, locals and visitors alike browse stalls offering everything from fresh fruits and vegetables to leather goods, clothing, and kitchenware. It is an excellent spot to pick up a wedge of **Grana Padano** cheese, a bottle of local olive oil, or a freshly baked loaf of **ciabatta**. Many of the products sold here come directly from nearby farms, making it an ideal place to experience the flavors of the region.

Beyond the weekly market, Sirmione hosts seasonal events and festivals that reflect its deep cultural heritage. One of the most anticipated celebrations is the **Festa di Santa Maria della Neve**, held every **August 5th**. This religious festival honors the patron saint of Sirmione with a procession through the town, accompanied by traditional music and a fireworks display over the lake. The event brings together residents and visitors for a day of community gatherings, church services, and lakeside celebrations.

During the Christmas season, **Mercatini di Natale** (Christmas markets) fill the town with festive charm. Stalls selling handmade crafts, holiday decorations, and seasonal treats line the streets, and the scent of **vin brulé** (mulled wine) fills the air. The floating nativity scene, displayed on the waters of Lake Garda near Scaliger Castle, adds a unique touch to the town's holiday traditions.

Spring and summer also bring their share of festivities. **Sirmione in Fiore**, a flower festival held in April, transforms the town with colorful displays, while **Notte Bianca**, or White Night, offers an evening of live music, street performances, and extended shop hours in July. These events highlight Sirmione's vibrant community spirit, providing visitors with a chance to celebrate alongside locals.

For those interested in the arts, the **Sirmione Book Festival** and **Lake Garda Music Festival** showcase literature and classical music in stunning settings, often within the castle grounds or near the lake. Attending one of these events is a way to see another side of Sirmione, one that embraces both its historical past and contemporary creativity.

## The Culinary Scene of Sirmione

Sirmione's food culture is deeply tied to its surroundings—Lake Garda's waters provide fresh fish, the nearby hills yield olives and wines, and the region's centuries-old culinary traditions influence every dish. Whether dining in a lakeside restaurant or sampling street food from a market stall, every meal tells a story of the land and its people.

One of the most iconic dishes in Sirmione is **Bigoli con le Sarde**, a pasta made with thick, whole-wheat noodles served with lake sardines, garlic, and olive oil. This dish is a reminder of the town's close relationship with the lake, where fishing has been a way of life for generations. Another local favorite is **Risotto con la Tinca**, a creamy risotto prepared with tench fish, which is particularly popular in the nearby town of Garda but also enjoyed in Sirmione's traditional kitchens.

Lake Garda is known for its **olive oil**, and Sirmione is no exception. The region's **extra virgin olive oil**, often labeled **Olio del Garda DOP**, is light and slightly fruity, making it perfect for drizzling over fresh salads or grilled fish. Many local restaurants serve it as a simple starter with freshly baked bread, allowing its delicate flavors to shine. For meat lovers, **Luganega** sausage, a specialty of Lombardy, appears on many menus, often grilled and served with polenta. Polenta itself is a staple in the region, sometimes replacing pasta as the base for rich, slow-cooked meat dishes like **Brasato al Vino Rosso**, a beef stew braised in red wine.

When it comes to wine, **Lugana** is the standout variety. This white wine, produced in the vineyards surrounding Sirmione, is crisp and aromatic, pairing perfectly with the area's fresh fish and light pastas. For those who prefer red wine, **Bardolino**—made just a short drive away—offers a smooth, fruity alternative. Many restaurants boast extensive wine lists featuring these local varieties, and a visit to a **Lugana winery** is a great way to learn more about the winemaking process.

No meal in Sirmione is complete without dessert. **Torta di Sbrisolona**, a crumbly almond cake originally from nearby Mantua, is a popular treat that pairs well with a glass of **Recioto**, a sweet dessert wine. For something lighter, **gelato** is a must-try, especially from one of the town's artisanal gelaterias that use fresh, local ingredients.

Dining in Sirmione is not just about the food—it is about the experience. Many of the town's best restaurants are set against the backdrop of the lake, with terraces that allow diners to enjoy their meal while watching the sunset. Whether in a fine-dining establishment or a casual trattoria, the flavors of Sirmione reflect its landscape, history, and traditions, making every bite a reflection of the town itself.

# Where to Stay and Dine

Sirmione offers a mix of traditional charm and modern comforts when it comes to dining and accommodations. From elegant lakeside restaurants serving regional specialties to boutique hotels with stunning views, the town caters to a wide range of tastes and budgets.

## Best Restaurants in Sirmione

Sirmione's dining scene is defined by its focus on fresh, locally sourced ingredients. Many restaurants take full advantage of their lakeside locations, offering open-air terraces where guests can enjoy regional dishes with a view. Below are some of the best restaurants in town, each known for its quality, ambiance, and authenticity.

### 1. Ristorante La Rucola 2.0

Address: Vicolo Strentelle, 21, 25019 Sirmione BS, Italy

GPS Coordinates: 45.4958° N, 10.6082° E

Specialties: Modern Italian cuisine with seasonal ingredients, fresh pasta, and an extensive wine list.

Why Visit? This Michelin-starred restaurant offers a refined dining experience in the heart of Sirmione's historic center, making it an excellent choice for a special night out.

### 2. Trattoria La Fiasca

Address: Via S. Salvatore, 5, 25019 Sirmione BS, Italy

GPS Coordinates: 45.4946° N, 10.6085° E

Specialties: Lake fish dishes, homemade pasta, and traditional Lombard cuisine.

Why Visit? A family-run trattoria with a warm atmosphere, known for its excellent service and authentic flavors.

### 3. Osteria al Torcol

Address: Via San Salvatore, 30, 25019 Sirmione BS, Italy

GPS Coordinates: 45.4950° N, 10.6090° E

Specialties: Grilled meats, risotto, and high-quality regional wines.

Why Visit? With a rustic-chic setting, this restaurant is ideal for those looking for hearty, flavorful Italian dishes.

### 4. Ristorante Risorgimento

Address: Piazza Carducci, 5, 25019 Sirmione BS, Italy

GPS Coordinates: 45.4947° N, 10.6079° E

Specialties: Gourmet seafood, lake fish, and premium cuts of meat.

Why Visit? One of the most historic restaurants in town, offering impeccable service and an extensive selection of fine wines.

### 5. Il Girasole

Address: Via Vittorio Emanuele, 72, 25019 Sirmione BS, Italy

GPS Coordinates: 45.4952° N, 10.6083° E

Specialties: Handmade pasta, grilled lake fish, and classic Italian desserts.

Why Visit? A well-loved spot with outdoor seating, perfect for a relaxed meal in the heart of the old town.

## Top-Rated Hotels and Accommodations

Sirmione offers a variety of accommodations, from luxury resorts with spa facilities to charming boutique hotels in the historic center. Here are some of the best places to stay, covering different price ranges and amenities.

### Luxury Hotels (€300+ per night)
### 1. Villa Cortine Palace Hotel

Address: Viale Gennari, 2, 25019 Sirmione BS, Italy

GPS Coordinates: 45.4972° N, 10.6084° E

Price Range: €400–€800 per night

Amenities: Private beach, outdoor pool, fine dining restaurant, lush gardens, and a bar with lake views.

Why Stay?: A five-star retreat offering exclusivity, elegance, and stunning lakefront views.

## 2. Grand Hotel Terme

Address: Viale Marconi, 7, 25019 Sirmione BS, Italy

GPS Coordinates: 45.4941° N, 10.6069° E

Price Range: €350–€700 per night

Amenities: Thermal spa, lakeside infinity pool, wellness center, and gourmet restaurant.

Why Stay?: A premier hotel known for its luxury spa treatments and breathtaking lake views.

## Mid-Range Hotels (€150–€300 per night)

### 1. Hotel Flaminia

Address: Piazza Flaminia, 8, 25019 Sirmione BS, Italy

GPS Coordinates: 45.4948° N, 10.6081° E

Price Range: €180–€300 per night

Amenities: Private sun terrace, restaurant, bar, and direct access to the lake.

Why Stay?: A charming lakefront hotel with modern comforts and an unbeatable location.

### 2. Hotel Olivi Spa & Natural Wellness

Address: Via San Pietro in Mavino, 5, 25019 Sirmione BS, Italy

GPS Coordinates: 45.4971° N, 10.6065° E

Price Range: €160–€280 per night

Amenities: Outdoor pool, spa, hot tub, and elegant rooms with balconies.

Why Stay? A relaxing escape just a short walk from the Grottoes of Catullus.

## Budget-Friendly Hotels (€80–€150 per night)

### 1. Hotel Marconi

Address: Via Vittorio Emanuele, 51, 25019 Sirmione BS, Italy

GPS Coordinates: 45.4950° N, 10.6077° E

Price Range: €90–€140 per night

Amenities: Lakeside breakfast terrace, free Wi-Fi, and family-friendly atmosphere.

Why Stay?: A great choice for travelers who want lake views at a reasonable price.

### 2. Hotel Serenella

Address: Via Punta Staffalo, 1, 25019 Sirmione BS, Italy

GPS Coordinates: 45.4976° N, 10.6075° E

Price Range: €100–€150 per night

Amenities: Outdoor swimming pool, cozy rooms, and proximity to the town center.

Why Stay?: A budget-friendly option with excellent service and a quiet location.

For those who prefer self-catering options, residences and vacation rentals are also widely available. Many apartments in Sirmione's historic center or along the peninsula's edge offer fully equipped kitchens, allowing guests to shop at local markets and cook their own meals.

With options ranging from five-star resorts to family-run guesthouses, Sirmione ensures that every traveler finds a comfortable and welcoming place to stay.

# CHAPTER 4: MALCESINE – A SCENIC ESCAPE

Malcesine is a town that blends natural beauty with a deep sense of history. Perched on the eastern shore of Lake Garda, it boasts medieval charm, dramatic mountain backdrops, and a lakeside atmosphere that makes it one of the most captivating spots around the lake. From cobbled streets lined with historic buildings to the breathtaking views from Monte Baldo, Malcesine offers a balance of adventure and relaxation.

## Breathtaking Views and Nature Walks

Malcesine is known for its stunning landscapes. The towering presence of Monte Baldo provides a striking contrast to the calm waters of Lake Garda, creating an environment that is both dramatic and serene. Walking through Malcesine means passing by ancient stone houses, lakeside promenades, and scenic trails leading to breathtaking viewpoints.

### Monte Baldo Cable Car: Panoramic Views

The Monte Baldo Cable Car is one of the most famous attractions in Malcesine, offering an opportunity to see the lake and surrounding mountains from an altitude of over 1,700 meters.

• • •

➡ **Location:** Via Navene Vecchia, 12, 37018 Malcesine VR, Italy
➡ **GPS Coordinates:** 45.7703° N, 10.8101° E
➡ **Opening Hours:** Varies by season; generally from 8:00 AM to 6:00 PM during peak months
➡ **Ticket Price:** Approximately €25 for a round trip (discounts available for children and groups)

The ride starts in Malcesine and takes passengers up to Tratto Spino, the highest accessible point on Monte Baldo. The cable car itself is designed with a rotating cabin, allowing everyone on board to enjoy a full 360-degree view during the ascent. As the town shrinks below, the vast blue of Lake Garda stretches out, framed by rugged cliffs and green slopes.

At the summit, hiking trails lead through alpine meadows filled with wildflowers in the warmer months and snow-covered ridges in winter. The views extend as far as the Dolomites on clear days, making it a favorite spot for photographers and nature enthusiasts. Paragliding is also popular here, with experienced pilots offering tandem flights for those seeking a more exhilarating way to experience the landscape.

For a more relaxed visit, there are mountain lodges where guests can enjoy local cuisine while taking in the view. A typical meal might include polenta with cheese, a hearty mountain stew, or a selection of cured meats and freshly baked bread.

The best times to take the cable car are early in the morning or late in the afternoon to avoid crowds. During peak season, lines can be long, so arriving before opening hours ensures a smoother experience.

## Historic Streets and Town Square

Malcesine's town center is a maze of medieval alleys, charming piazzas, and centuries-old buildings that reflect its deep-rooted history. Walking through these streets is like stepping back in time, with each stone pathway and wooden-shuttered house telling a story of the past. The town's layout, shaped by the natural contours of the land, leads gently down to the waterfront, where the lake adds a sense of serenity to the historic atmosphere.

At the heart of Malcesine lies **Piazza Statuto**, the town's main square. This open space has long been a gathering point for locals and visitors alike. During the day, it is filled with people sipping espresso at outdoor cafés, browsing small shops, or taking a break on one of the stone benches. In the evening, the square takes on a different character as restaurants fill with diners, street performers entertain passersby, and the warm glow of lanterns reflects off the surrounding buildings. The square is also the site of seasonal markets and occasional festivals, bringing an added vibrancy to the town's social life.

Surrounding Piazza Statuto, the streets weave in various directions, offering endless opportunities for discovery. Many of these lanes remain largely unchanged since medieval times, retaining their original stonework and narrow dimensions. The architecture is distinctly Venetian in style, a reminder of Malcesine's time under the Republic of Venice. Some buildings feature frescoes that have faded over the centuries but still hint at their former beauty. Others are adorned with climbing vines and flower boxes, adding a natural touch to the historic setting.

One of the most charming aspects of Malcesine's old town is the abundance of **small, family-run shops**. These stores sell everything from handcrafted leather goods to locally produced olive oil, wine, and honey. Artisans display their work in small studios, offering handmade ceramics and paintings inspired by Lake Garda's landscapes. Unlike larger tourist-heavy destinations, many of these businesses have been in the same families for generations, maintaining a sense of tradition in their craftsmanship.

A short walk from the main square leads to **Porto Vecchio**, the old harbor. This picturesque spot is framed by colorful buildings, fishing boats, and a few lakeside restaurants with outdoor terraces. It serves as both a working port and a scenic viewpoint, where visitors can watch the gentle movements of the lake while enjoying a meal or a glass of local wine. Ferries depart from here to other towns along the lake, making it a key location for those looking to explore further.

Among Malcesine's most historically significant structures is **Palazzo dei Capitani**, an elegant Venetian-style palace that once served as the administrative center when the town was under Venetian rule. Built between the 13th and 15th centuries, the palace features intricate Gothic windows, frescoed ceilings, and a beautiful garden that overlooks the lake. While much of its interior remains private, visitors can step inside certain areas to admire the craftsmanship and history preserved within its walls.

Another notable landmark tucked away in Malcesine's winding streets is **Chiesa di Santo Stefano**, an 18th-century church that offers a peaceful retreat from the busier parts of town. Though modest in size, its Baroque interior is richly decorated with frescoes, gilded accents, and an ornate altar. The church is still active, hosting regular services and religious festivals throughout the year.

For those who enjoy discovering quieter corners, Malcesine offers several hidden courtyards and side alleys that reveal unexpected gems. Some alleys lead to small squares with stone fountains, while others open up to terraces with breathtaking lake views. Locals often recommend wandering without a plan, allowing the streets to lead the way and discovering the town's lesser-known spots along the journey. The town's historical character is further emphasized by its connection to literary figures, most notably Johann Wolfgang von Goethe, who visited Malcesine in 1786. During his Italian Journey, Goethe was captivated by the beauty of the town and famously sketched Scaliger Castle, an act that nearly got him arrested on suspicion of espionage. Today, a plaque near the castle commemorates his visit, marking the town's place in European literary history.

Malcesine's old town is not just a place to see; it is a place to experience. Every cobblestone street, wooden balcony, and lakeside bench holds a connection to the past. The rhythm of daily life here, set against the backdrop of Lake Garda and Monte Baldo, makes it one of the most captivating spots in the region.

## Culinary Highlights

Malcesine, nestled along the shores of Lake Garda, offers a culinary scene that reflects its rich history and the abundance of the region. From gourmet dining experiences to cozy cafés and wine bars, the town caters to a variety of palates, ensuring that every meal becomes a memorable part of your journey.

## Gourmet Restaurants in Malcesine

For those seeking an elevated dining experience, Malcesine boasts several gourmet restaurants that combine traditional Italian flavors with innovative culinary techniques. Here are some notable establishments:

⇨ **La Bottega del Vino**

- ❖ 🏠*Address:* Corso Giuseppe Garibaldi, 19, 37018 Malcesine VR, Italy
- ❖ 📍 *GPS Coordinates:* 45.7595° N, 10.8110° E
- ❖ 📝*Overview:* Known for its extensive wine selection and a menu that highlights local produce, La Bottega del Vino offers a cozy yet sophisticated atmosphere. Dishes range from classic pasta to carefully crafted meat and seafood options, all designed to pair perfectly with their curated wine list.

⇨ **Ristorante La Pace**

- ❖ 🏠*Address:* Piazza Statuto, 37018 Malcesine VR, Italy
- ❖ 📍 *GPS Coordinates:* 45.7590° N, 10.8115° E
- ❖ 📝*Overview:* Situated in the heart of Malcesine, Ristorante La Pace provides diners with stunning lake views and a menu rich in seafood specialties. The fresh catch of the day is a highlight, prepared with regional herbs and accompanied by locally sourced vegetables.

⇨ **Vecchia Malcesine**

- ❖ 🏠*Address:* Via Pisort, 6, 37018 Malcesine VR, Italy
- ❖ 📍 *GPS Coordinates:* 45.7598° N, 10.8122° E
- ❖ 📝*Overview:* This Michelin-starred restaurant offers a modern twist on traditional Italian cuisine. Chef Leandro Luppi crafts tasting menus that take guests on a culinary journey, showcasing seasonal ingredients and innovative techniques. Reservations are highly recommended due to its esteemed reputation.

⇨ **Al Gondoliere**

- ❖ 🏠*Address:* Piazza Vittorio Emanuele, 6, 37018 Malcesine VR, Italy

- ❖    *GPS Coordinates:* 45.7592° N, 10.8118° E
- ❖    *Overview:* A family-run establishment, Al Gondoliere is celebrated for its warm hospitality and a menu that emphasizes regional dishes. Homemade pastas, risottos, and a selection of fine wines make it a favorite among both locals and visitors.

➡ **Ristorante al Corsaro**
- ❖    *Address:* Via Paina, 17, 37018 Malcesine VR, Italy
- ❖    *GPS Coordinates:* 45.7601° N, 10.8125° E
- ❖    *Overview:* Nestled near the Scaliger Castle, Ristorante al Corsaro offers a romantic setting with panoramic lake views. The menu features a blend of traditional and contemporary dishes, with an emphasis on fresh, local ingredients.

---

## Cozy Cafés and Wine Bars

Beyond formal dining, Malcesine's charm is amplified by its array of intimate cafés and wine bars, perfect for a relaxed afternoon or evening.

➡ **Dodo Café**
*Address:* Via Gardesana, 226, 37018 Malcesine VR, Italy
*GPS Coordinates:* 45.7587° N, 10.8109° E
*Overview:* A popular spot for both locals and tourists, Dodo Café offers a selection of pastries, light bites, and an impressive coffee menu. Its lakeside location makes it an ideal place to unwind and enjoy the serene views.

➡ **Caffè San Marco**
*Address:* Piazza Guglielmo Marconi, 15, 37018 Malcesine VR, Italy
*GPS Coordinates:* 45.7593° N, 10.8117° E
*Overview:* Known for its artisanal gelato and freshly brewed espresso, Caffè San Marco provides a cozy

atmosphere right in the town center. It's a perfect stop for a mid-morning treat or an afternoon refreshment.

### ⇨ La Bottega del Vino

*Address:* Corso Giuseppe Garibaldi, 19, 37018 Malcesine VR, Italy

*GPS Coordinates:* 45.7595° N, 10.8110° E

*Overview:* In addition to being a gourmet restaurant, La Bottega del Vino operates as a wine bar, offering an extensive selection of regional and international wines. Guests can enjoy wine tastings accompanied by curated cheese and charcuterie boards.

### ⇨ Paragliding Snack Bar

*Address:* Via Navene Vecchia, 10, 37018 Malcesine VR, Italy

*GPS Coordinates:* 45.7700° N, 10.8100° E

*Overview:* A unique spot favored by adventure enthusiasts, this snack bar offers simple meals, refreshing drinks, and a chance to watch paragliders take off and land. The casual setting and friendly staff make it a great place to relax after outdoor activities.

### ⇨ Bar Al Porto

*Address:* Via Porto Vecchio, 5, 37018 Malcesine VR, Italy

*GPS Coordinates:* 45.7591° N, 10.8116° E

*Overview:* Located by the old harbor, Bar Al Porto provides a laid-back environment to enjoy a selection of local wines, cocktails, and light snacks. The outdoor seating offers picturesque views of the lake and passing boats.

Malcesine's culinary landscape is a testament to its rich cultural heritage and the natural bounty of the Lake Garda region. Whether you're indulging in a gourmet meal or sipping a glass of wine at a cozy café, the town offers a diverse range of experiences to satisfy every palate.

# Shopping and Local Crafts

Malcesine's charm extends beyond its picturesque landscapes to a vibrant shopping scene that reflects the town's rich cultural heritage. From bustling artisan markets to quaint boutiques, visitors can immerse themselves in local craftsmanship and find unique souvenirs to commemorate their Lake Garda experience.

## Artisan Markets and Souvenirs

Shopping in Malcesine is as much about the experience as it is about the items you take home. The town's artisan markets and small specialty shops reflect centuries-old traditions, with local craftsmen and food producers bringing their expertise to the forefront. Whether browsing for handmade ceramics, regional olive oil, or locally produced textiles, every market stall and boutique tells a story of Malcesine's cultural heritage.

### The Weekly Market: A Local Tradition

Every Saturday morning, Malcesine's weekly market transforms part of the town into a lively hub of activity. Locals and visitors gather early to explore the wide range of goods available, from fresh produce to artisanal crafts. The market runs from **8:00 AM to 2:00 PM** and stretches along the lakefront promenade, spilling into the town's smaller squares and side streets.

Here, visitors can find locally sourced cheeses, cured meats, and bread, with many products coming from small farms in the surrounding hills. One of the standout offerings is Monte Baldo honey, a golden, aromatic honey produced from wildflowers that thrive in the alpine meadows of Monte Baldo. This delicacy is prized for its rich floral notes and is often sold alongside homemade jams and preserves.

For those interested in regional crafts, the market features vendors selling handwoven textiles, wood carvings, and pottery. Many of the tablecloths and scarves on display are made using traditional techniques passed down through generations. The intricate embroidery and fine fabrics make them ideal gifts or personal keepsakes.

One of the most popular sections of the market is dedicated to leather goods. Small workshops in the region specialize in high-quality leather craftsmanship, producing belts, handbags, and wallets in a variety of styles. The soft, durable leather used in these items ensures they last for years, making them a worthwhile investment.

## Locally Produced Olive Oil: A Taste of Lake Garda

Olive oil production around Lake Garda has a history dating back to Roman times, and Malcesine remains one of the best places to sample and purchase high-quality extra virgin olive oil. Many small shops in town specialize in cold-pressed olive oil made from centuries-old olive groves in the surrounding hills.

Visitors looking for authentic Olio del Garda DOP (Protected Designation of Origin) can find it in local specialty stores or at the weekly market. This olive oil is known for its delicate, slightly fruity flavor, making it ideal for salads, drizzling over fresh bread, or pairing with grilled fish. Some producers also sell flavored olive oils, infused with ingredients like lemon, rosemary, or chili pepper, providing unique variations on the classic staple.

Tasting sessions are often available, allowing visitors to sample different varieties and learn about the traditional pressing process used in local mills. Many producers adhere to organic farming practices, ensuring that their olive oil maintains the purity and authenticity that has defined the region's agricultural traditions for centuries.

## Handcrafted Ceramics and Pottery

Malcesine is home to a small but dedicated community of ceramic artists who create hand-painted pottery inspired by the landscapes of Lake Garda. These artisans use age-old techniques to craft plates, bowls, and decorative tiles, each piece showcasing vibrant colors and intricate patterns.

Shops in the historic center display rows of ceramic vases, espresso cups, and serving platters, often decorated with motifs of olive branches, lemons, or the shimmering waters of the lake. Some artisans also produce custom pieces, allowing visitors to request personalized designs or inscriptions to commemorate their time in Malcesine.

One particularly sought-after souvenir is the majolica tile, a traditional form of Italian pottery known for its bright colors and detailed glazing. These tiles are often used as decorative wall pieces or trivets for kitchens and dining tables.

**Locally Made Jewelry and Accessories**
For those looking for something more personal, Malcesine's small jewelry workshops offer a range of handcrafted accessories, from silver bracelets to glass bead necklaces. Many jewelers take inspiration from the natural beauty of Lake Garda, incorporating semi-precious stones and locally sourced materials into their designs.
Lava stone beads from Monte Baldo, Murano glass pendants, and silver charms shaped like the lake's outline are just a few of the unique items available. These handmade pieces make meaningful gifts and are a way to carry a small piece of Malcesine wherever you go.

**Wine and Spirits: A Taste of the Region**
No visit to Malcesine is complete without sampling some of the region's finest wines and liqueurs. Many shops specialize in Lugana and Bardolino wines, both produced in vineyards around Lake Garda. Lugana is a crisp white wine with floral and citrus notes, while Bardolino is a light red with a refreshing fruitiness.
Another popular product is Limoncino del Garda, a variation of the famous Limoncello produced using lemons grown around the lake. Its sweet, tangy flavor makes it a favorite souvenir, often sold in beautifully decorated bottles. Some distilleries also produce Grappa, a traditional Italian spirit made from grape pomace, which is best enjoyed as a digestif after a meal.
Many wine shops offer tasting sessions, allowing visitors to sample different varieties before choosing a bottle to take home. Knowledgeable shop owners are happy to explain the differences between vintages and recommend pairings based on individual tastes.

**Handmade Wooden Crafts and Sculptures**
Woodworking has been an important craft in the region for centuries, and Malcesine's artisan markets often feature hand-carved wooden sculptures, kitchen utensils, and decorative items. Some artisans

create miniature boats and lake-inspired carvings, while others specialize in functional pieces like olive wood cutting boards and serving spoons.

For those interested in more intricate works, some shops sell handcrafted nativity scenes and detailed model replicas of local landmarks, including Scaliger Castle and Monte Baldo. These carefully carved pieces reflect the dedication and artistry of Malcesine's woodworkers.

Malcesine's artisan markets and specialty shops offer more than just souvenirs—they provide a direct connection to the town's history, culture, and craftsmanship. Each item, whether it is a bottle of locally pressed olive oil, a hand-painted ceramic plate, or a leather-bound notebook, carries with it the essence of the region. Shopping here is not about mass-produced goods but about supporting local artisans and taking home a piece of Malcesine's story.

## Boutique Shopping Experiences

Malcesine offers more than just stunning lake views and historical landmarks—it's also a fantastic place for boutique shopping. Unlike the larger commercial shopping districts found in Verona or Milan, Malcesine's shopping scene is more intimate, featuring small, locally owned boutiques that showcase carefully curated selections of clothing, accessories, home décor, and artisanal goods. Wandering through the charming cobbled streets, you'll find unique shops that reflect the character and craftsmanship of the region.

One of the best things about boutique shopping in Malcesine is the variety of stores catering to different tastes and preferences. Many boutiques specialize in high-quality Italian fashion, offering stylish clothing, leather goods, and handmade jewelry. These shops often feature items crafted by local designers, giving visitors the opportunity to purchase one-of-a-kind pieces that can't be found anywhere else.

One standout boutique is located near the town square, offering a collection of linen and cotton clothing designed for the relaxed yet elegant Italian lifestyle. The garments are typically made with breathable fabrics, perfect for Lake Garda's warm summers. Soft pastel dresses, stylish scarves, and lightweight linen trousers are some of the staple pieces available. The boutique's owner, a Malcesine native, carefully selects each item to reflect both traditional Italian craftsmanship and modern fashion trends.

For those who appreciate fine leather goods, there are several small leather shops scattered throughout the old town. These boutiques offer handmade belts, handbags, and wallets crafted using traditional Italian techniques. Some even provide custom engraving or embossing services, allowing visitors to personalize their purchases. Italian leather is known for its durability and softness, making these items a great investment and a meaningful souvenir from Malcesine.

Jewelry lovers will also find plenty to admire in Malcesine's boutiques. Some shops specialize in Murano glass jewelry, a Venetian tradition that dates back centuries. These delicate, colorful pieces are made using techniques that create intricate patterns and striking color combinations. Other jewelry boutiques focus on silver and gold designs, many of which are inspired by the natural beauty of Lake Garda. From simple, elegant pieces to more elaborate statement jewelry, there's something for every taste.

Home décor stores in Malcesine also stand out for their selection of hand-painted ceramics, textiles, and locally crafted wooden items. Some boutiques sell decorative plates, bowls, and vases featuring intricate floral or geometric patterns, while others offer handwoven textiles such as tablecloths, runners, and cushion covers. These pieces not only make excellent souvenirs but also bring a touch of Italian craftsmanship into any home.

In addition to fashion and home décor, Malcesine is also home to specialty stores that sell gourmet products such as olive oil, truffle-infused delicacies, and locally made spirits. Some boutiques focus on regional flavors, offering beautifully packaged bottles of extra virgin olive oil produced from the ancient groves surrounding Lake Garda. Others sell artisan chocolates, honey, and jams, all made with high-quality local ingredients. These gourmet items make excellent gifts or personal treats to enjoy after the trip.

What makes boutique shopping in Malcesine particularly enjoyable is the personal experience. Many of these stores are family-owned, and the shopkeepers take pride in sharing their knowledge and passion for their products. Visitors are often welcomed with friendly conversation and, in some cases, even a small sample of their goods. The relaxed atmosphere of Malcesine allows shoppers to take their time browsing, appreciating the craftsmanship, and learning about the history behind each piece.

Shopping in Malcesine is not about rushing from store to store; it's about strolling through the town's charming streets, discovering hidden gems, and enjoying the process of finding something special. The experience is far removed from the hurried pace of large shopping centers, making it an enjoyable and memorable part of any visit to Lake Garda.

# CHAPTER 5: RIVA DEL GARDA – THE OUTDOOR ENTHUSIAST'S HAVEN

## Notable Landmarks

Riva del Garda is a destination that blends history, culture, and breathtaking scenery. Among its most notable landmarks are sites that tell the story of its past while offering spectacular views and deep cultural significance. Visitors walking through the town will quickly notice the well-preserved architecture, medieval fortifications, and museums that give insight into Riva's role as a crossroads of trade, military strategy, and artistic expression.

### The Bastione: A Historic Fortress with a View

Perched on the slopes of Mount Rocchetta, the Bastione is one of Riva del Garda's most iconic historical sites. Built in the early 16th century by the Venetians, this stone fortress was constructed to defend the town from invaders. The Republic of Venice, which controlled much of northern Italy during this period, recognized Riva's strategic importance and reinforced its defenses accordingly. The Bastione was a key part of this system, standing as a silent guardian over the town and the waters of Lake Garda.

The fortress was originally much larger, but in 1703, during the War of the Spanish Succession, French forces led by General Vendôme destroyed much of its structure. What remains today is a fascinating ruin that still carries the weight of history in its weathered stone walls. The remnants of its circular tower and outer fortifications offer visitors a glimpse into its former grandeur, while the climb to reach it provides a rewarding experience for those interested in both history and scenic landscapes.

**What to Do at the Bastione**

⇨ **Take the Funicular** – A modern glass funicular now makes reaching the Bastione easy and enjoyable. The ride offers panoramic views of Riva del Garda and Lake Garda as it ascends the hillside.

➡ **Enjoy the Scenic Hike** – Those who prefer a more active experience can follow the well-maintained walking trail up the hillside. The hike takes about 20–30 minutes and offers stunning viewpoints along the way.

➡ **Relax at the Café** – At the top, a small café next to the ruins serves drinks and snacks with breathtaking lake views. It's an excellent place to sit and appreciate the surroundings.

➡ **Photography and Sightseeing** – The Bastione's location makes it one of the best spots for capturing views of Riva del Garda, the northern shores of the lake, and the surrounding mountains.

### How to Get There

➡ On Foot – The hiking trail to the Bastione begins in Riva del Garda's town center. Follow the signs near the waterfront leading toward Mount Rocchetta.

➡ By Funicular – The funicular station is located at Via Monte Oro, 26, 38066 Riva del Garda TN, Italy. The ride to the top takes just a few minutes.

➡ GPS Coordinates – 45.8854° N, 10.8421° E

## MAG Museum: The Cultural Heart of Riva

The Museo Alto Garda (MAG) is the premier cultural institution in Riva del Garda, housed in the medieval Rocca di Riva, a castle surrounded by water on three sides. The Rocca itself is a landmark, dating back to the 12th century when it served as a defensive fortress for the ruling families of the region. Over time, it evolved from a military stronghold into a civic institution, and today, it stands as a guardian of the town's artistic and historical heritage.

The museum's exhibitions are carefully curated to highlight the diverse influences that have shaped Riva del Garda and the surrounding Trentino region. One of its most compelling sections focuses on the town's role in trade and military conflicts throughout history. Maps, artifacts, and interactive displays illustrate how Riva was a key point of passage between northern and southern Europe, making it a contested and valuable location for centuries.

Another significant part of the museum is its collection of art from the 19th and 20th centuries. Many of the paintings depict Lake Garda in various seasons, capturing its changing moods and colors. Artists from across Europe have long been drawn to the lake's dramatic landscape, and their works provide a historical record of how Riva and its surroundings have evolved over time. Visitors with an appreciation for Italian and Alpine art will find this section particularly rewarding.

In addition to its historical and artistic exhibits, the MAG Museum also dedicates space to the region's natural history. The geological formations around Lake Garda, including the dramatic cliffs and glacial valleys, are explained through engaging multimedia displays. This part of the museum is especially interesting for those curious about how the lake itself was formed and how the unique microclimate supports diverse flora and fauna.

For those visiting with children, the museum offers hands-on workshops and interactive activities designed to engage younger audiences. These sessions bring history to life through storytelling, crafts, and educational games. The museum staff frequently updates these programs, ensuring that there is always something new for returning visitors.

## What to Do at the MAG Museum

⇨ **Explore the Castle and Museum** – The Rocca di Riva itself is worth exploring, with its medieval architecture and waterside location adding to the charm of the museum visit.

⇨ **Learn About Riva's History** – The exhibits cover everything from ancient settlements to modern-day Riva del Garda, making it an excellent place for history lovers.

⇨ **Admire Regional Artwork** – The museum houses works from local and international artists who have been inspired by Lake Garda's landscape.

⇨ **Visit the Natural History Section** – Learn about the geological and ecological features that make this region unique.

➯ **Attend a Workshop or Guided Tour** – The museum frequently hosts educational events and guided tours, which can provide deeper insight into the exhibits.

**How to Get There**

➯ By Foot – The museum is centrally located in Riva del Garda's historic town center, making it easily accessible on foot from most hotels and accommodations.

➯ By Car – There are parking areas nearby, including the Terme Romane Parking Garage, about a five-minute walk away.

➯ By Public Transport – Buses from other Lake Garda towns stop at the main station in Riva del Garda, from where it is a short walk to the museum.

➯ Address – Rocca di Riva, Piazza Cesare Battisti, 3/A, 38066 Riva del Garda TN, Italy

➯ GPS Coordinates – 45.8849° N, 10.8416° E

# Food and Wine Scene

Riva del Garda offers a rich culinary landscape that reflects both the local Trentino traditions and the Mediterranean influences of Lake Garda. Freshwater fish, mountain cheeses, and olive oil are staples of the region's cuisine, while the area's unique climate allows for the production of excellent wines and olive oils. Dining here is not just about eating; it's about experiencing the flavors that define the region, crafted with generations of expertise.

## Traditional Garda Cuisine

Riva del Garda's cuisine is a reflection of its unique location, where Alpine traditions meet Mediterranean influences. The region's fertile land, freshwater lakes, and rolling hills provide an abundance of ingredients that have shaped local food for centuries. The culinary offerings here are deeply rooted in tradition, showcasing simple yet flavorful dishes that highlight high-quality, seasonal ingredients.

## Lake Fish: A Staple of Garda Cuisine

The waters of Lake Garda provide an essential source of food for the communities along its shores. Freshwater fish plays a significant role in local dishes, with species like **trout, perch, whitefish (*lavarello*), and sardines** commonly appearing on menus. One of the most popular dishes is **Bigoli con le Sarde**, a pasta made with thick, whole-wheat strands served in a savory sauce of lake sardines, garlic, and parsley. The sardines are preserved using an age-old salting technique that enhances their rich, umami flavor.

Another must-try dish is **Risotto al Persico**, a creamy risotto made with locally caught perch. The fish is lightly pan-seared and added to the risotto just before serving, creating a delicate yet satisfying dish. This pairs well with the region's crisp white wines, which balance out the richness of the risotto.

For those who enjoy grilled fish, **Coregone alla Griglia** is a simple but delicious preparation. Whitefish, known as *coregone*, is grilled with olive oil, lemon, and herbs, allowing its mild flavor to shine. It is often served with polenta, a staple side dish in northern Italy that complements the delicate texture of the fish.

## Mountain-Inspired Dishes and Cured Meats

Moving away from the lake, the cuisine of Riva del Garda incorporates influences from the mountains that surround it. One of the region's most iconic specialties is **Carne Salada**, a cured beef dish that originated in Trentino. The meat is seasoned with salt, pepper, bay leaves, and juniper berries, then left to cure for several weeks. It is served in two ways: raw in thin slices, similar to carpaccio, or lightly grilled for a more robust flavor. It pairs exceptionally well with Fasòi, a hearty bean stew that complements the saltiness of the meat.

Cured meats are an integral part of Garda cuisine, with specialties such as Speck, a smoked ham with a distinct flavor, and Luganega, a coiled sausage with a mildly spiced taste. These meats are often served as antipasti alongside cheeses and local bread, making for a perfect appetizer.

For a warming mountain dish, **Gnocchi di Malga** is a must-try. These hearty potato dumplings, originally from the Alpine pastures, are served with melted butter, sage, and grated Trentingrana cheese. The simplicity of the dish highlights the quality of the ingredients, creating a rich and satisfying meal.

### Polenta: The Versatile Side Dish

No meal in Riva del Garda is complete without polenta. This cornmeal dish has been a staple in northern Italy for centuries and is served in various forms. **Polenta e Gorgonzola** is a popular preparation, where creamy Gorgonzola cheese is melted over soft polenta, creating a rich and comforting dish. Another variation is **Polenta Carbonera**, which includes bits of pancetta and cheese, giving it a smoky, savory flavor. Polenta also pairs beautifully with slow-cooked meats like Brasato al Vino Rosso, a beef dish braised in red wine until tender. The combination of the soft, creamy polenta and the deep flavors of the wine-infused beef creates a meal that is both rustic and refined.

### Olive Oil: Liquid Gold of Lake Garda

Lake Garda is home to some of the northernmost olive groves in Europe, producing a highly sought-after olive oil known as **Extra Virgin Olive Oil DOP Garda Trentino**. This olive oil is lighter and more delicate than its southern counterparts, with a smooth, slightly sweet taste. It is used generously in local dishes, from drizzling over grilled fish to enhancing the flavor of salads and vegetables.

Many restaurants and agriturismos in the region offer olive oil tastings, allowing visitors to experience the nuances of this prized ingredient. The oil's mild fruitiness and peppery finish make it an excellent addition to simple dishes like Bruschetta al Pomodoro, where toasted bread is topped with fresh tomatoes, garlic, and basil, then finished with a generous drizzle of olive oil.

### Cheese and Dairy Delicacies

Cheese lovers will find plenty to enjoy in Riva del Garda, as the region produces several outstanding varieties. **Trentingrana** is a hard cheese similar to Parmigiano-Reggiano, known for its nutty, slightly salty taste. It is often grated over pasta and risotto or enjoyed on its own with honey and walnuts.

Another local favorite is **Puzzone di Moena**, a semi-soft cheese with a strong aroma and a rich, buttery flavor. This cheese is commonly used in cooking, particularly in Canederli, which are bread dumplings mixed with cheese, speck, and herbs.

**Traditional Desserts and Sweet Treats**
To end a meal on a sweet note, Riva del Garda offers several traditional desserts that reflect the area's diverse culinary heritage. **Torta di Fregoloti** is a classic almond and butter cake with a crumbly texture, often served with a glass of dessert wine. The cake's rich, nutty flavor makes it a satisfying treat after a meal.

For a dessert with Austrian influence, **Strudel di Mele** is a must-try. This apple strudel is made with thin layers of pastry wrapped around cinnamon-spiced apples, raisins, and nuts. It is typically served warm with a dusting of powdered sugar and a scoop of vanilla gelato.

Another unique dessert is **Zelten**, a dense fruitcake traditionally enjoyed during the holiday season. Made with dried fruits, nuts, and honey, this sweet bread is packed with flavor and pairs wonderfully with a glass of local Moscato wine.

**A Culinary Experience Rooted in Tradition**
The cuisine of Riva del Garda is more than just a collection of dishes—it's a reflection of the land, history, and traditions of the region. From the delicate flavors of lake fish to the hearty dishes of the mountains, every meal tells a story of the people who have lived and cooked here for generations. Dining in Riva del Garda is an experience that blends fresh, local ingredients with time-honored recipes, creating meals that are both comforting and deeply satisfying.

## Wine Tasting Experiences in Riva del Garda

Wine culture in Riva del Garda is deeply rooted in the region's history, shaped by its mild climate and fertile soil. The northern shores of Lake Garda provide the perfect conditions for cultivating a variety of grapes, resulting in wines that are both refined and distinctive. From crisp whites to full-bodied reds, the area offers something for every palate. Visiting local wineries and wine bars provides an opportunity to experience the craftsmanship behind these wines, learn about traditional winemaking techniques, and enjoy the stunning landscapes that surround the vineyards.

## The Unique Terroir of Garda Trentino

The combination of Alpine breezes, Mediterranean sun, and mineral-rich soil gives Garda Trentino wines a unique profile. The grapes grown here benefit from the cool mountain air, which preserves their acidity and freshness, while the warm lake climate enhances their ripeness and complexity. The result is wines with a balanced character, often featuring floral and citrus notes in whites and deep berry flavors in reds.

One of the most famous grapes in the region is Nosiola, a native white variety known for its light, aromatic qualities and slight hazelnut undertone. This grape is also used to produce the renowned Vino Santo, a sweet wine made by drying the grapes before fermentation to concentrate their sugars.

Another important variety is Marzemino, a red grape that thrives in the volcanic soils of Trentino. Marzemino wines are medium-bodied, with fruity and floral notes, making them an excellent pairing for local dishes like cured meats and aged cheeses.

## Wineries and Vineyards to Visit

Several wineries near Riva del Garda offer guided tours and tastings, allowing visitors to learn about the region's winemaking traditions while sampling a range of wines. Many of these wineries are family-run, maintaining a deep connection to the land and a commitment to quality.

One such winery is **Cantina Toblino**, located a short drive from Riva del Garda. This historic winery is known for producing **Nosiola** and **Vino Santo**, both of which reflect the essence of the region. The guided tour includes a walk through the vineyards, a visit to the cellars, and a tasting session featuring a selection of their best wines.

Another excellent stop is **Agraria Riva del Garda**, a cooperative that produces both wine and olive oil. Their wine tastings often include a pairing with local cheeses and cured meats, highlighting how the flavors complement each other. The facility also features a well-stocked shop where visitors can purchase bottles to take home.

For those looking to explore biodynamic winemaking, **Pisoni Winery** offers an insightful experience. This family-run estate follows organic and sustainable practices, focusing on natural fermentation and minimal intervention. Their tasting sessions provide a deeper understanding of how environmental factors influence wine production, making it a fascinating visit for wine enthusiasts.

## Wine Bars and Tasting Rooms

If visiting a vineyard isn't on the agenda, several wine bars in Riva del Garda offer curated tasting experiences that showcase the best local and regional wines. These venues provide an intimate setting to enjoy a glass while learning about the unique characteristics of each variety.

**Enoteca La Nicchia** is a popular choice for wine lovers, featuring an extensive selection of Garda Trentino wines. The knowledgeable staff can guide visitors through different tastings, offering insights into each wine's flavor profile and pairing suggestions. Their selection includes both well-known labels and small-batch wines that are harder to find outside the region.

Another excellent spot is **Osteria La Contrada**, a charming wine bar that pairs local wines with small plates of regional specialties. Their focus is on natural and organic wines, often sourced from small producers who prioritize traditional methods. The cozy ambiance makes it a great place to unwind and savor the depth of Garda's winemaking heritage.

## Wine Festivals and Events

Throughout the year, Riva del Garda hosts several wine-related events that celebrate the region's viticultural excellence. These festivals provide a fantastic opportunity to sample a wide range of wines, meet local producers, and enjoy the festive atmosphere.

One of the most anticipated events is **DiVinNosiola**, held in the spring to honor the Nosiola grape and the production of Vino Santo. The festival includes tastings, vineyard tours, and cultural events that highlight the historical significance of this unique wine.

In the summer, many wineries participate in open-cellar events, where visitors can tour multiple estates in a single day, enjoying tastings and learning about the different approaches to winemaking. These events often include live music, food pairings, and the chance to meet the winemakers themselves.

For those visiting in the autumn, the harvest season brings a variety of activities, from grape-picking experiences to special tasting menus that celebrate the new vintage. This is an excellent time to visit, as the vineyards are full of life, and the weather is perfect for exploring.

**Pairing Garda Wines with Local Cuisine**

Wine tasting in Riva del Garda isn't just about sampling different vintages—it's also about understanding how wine complements the region's cuisine. The local whites, like Nosiola and Chardonnay, pair beautifully with lake fish and delicate pasta dishes, while reds such as Marzemino and Teroldego are excellent with grilled meats and aged cheeses.

For a perfect pairing, try a glass of Vino Santo with a slice of Torta di Fregoloti, a crumbly almond cake that enhances the wine's rich sweetness. Similarly, a full-bodied Teroldego pairs wonderfully with Carne Salada, as its tannins balance the saltiness of the cured meat.

Experiencing the wines of Riva del Garda is as much about the culture as it is about the flavors. Each glass tells a story of the land, the climate, and the generations of winemakers who have perfected their craft.

# CHAPTER 6: DESENZANO DEL GARDA – A VIBRANT LAKESIDE TOWN

## Historic and Cultural Attractions

Desenzano del Garda is a town where history and modern life blend effortlessly. The charming streets, ancient ruins, and well-preserved landmarks tell the story of its rich past, from Roman settlements to medieval fortifications. Strolling through its historic center, visitors can see how different eras have left their mark on the town's architecture and cultural heritage.

One of the standout features of Desenzano is its connection to the Roman era. The town was once an important trading post, benefiting from its prime location on Lake Garda. Over the centuries, it evolved into a key defensive stronghold during medieval times before becoming the lively town it is today.

## Desenzano Castle: A Timeless Landmark

Perched atop a gentle hill overlooking the town and the waters of Lake Garda, Desenzano Castle is a striking reminder of the medieval past of Desenzano del Garda. While the castle no longer serves its original defensive purpose, its imposing walls, ancient towers, and panoramic views make it one of the most significant historical landmarks in the area.

### A Fortress with a Purpose

Desenzano Castle dates back to the 10th century, a time when the threat of barbarian invasions loomed over northern Italy. The fortress was initially constructed to offer protection against raiders who frequently attacked settlements along the lake. Over the centuries, the castle was expanded and reinforced, particularly during the 13th and 14th centuries, when Desenzano became an important military outpost under the rule of the Scaliger family from Verona.

The strategic location of the castle made it an ideal stronghold. From its elevated position, defenders could monitor the surrounding landscape and prepare for any approaching threats. The thick stone walls and fortified towers ensured the safety of the local population, who would often seek refuge within its walls during times of conflict.

### Architecture and Features

Though parts of the castle have undergone restoration, much of the original medieval structure remains intact. The outer walls, built with large stone blocks, encircle the fortress and create a sense of grandeur as visitors approach. The entrance, featuring a large arched gateway, leads into the castle's interior, where remnants of ancient living quarters and military facilities can still be seen.

One of the most impressive features is the main tower, which stands tall at the highest point of the fortress. This tower once served as a watchtower, providing a 360-degree view of the lake and the surrounding countryside. Today, visitors can climb to the top and enjoy breathtaking views that stretch as far as the distant mountains. The climb is relatively easy, with well-maintained steps leading to the summit.

The castle's inner courtyard, which was once used for military drills and community gatherings, has been repurposed into a venue for cultural events. Throughout the year, the space hosts concerts, theater performances, and historical reenactments, bringing a vibrant energy to the ancient walls.

## A Historical Timeline

Over the centuries, the role of Desenzano Castle evolved. By the 16th century, as the threat of invasions declined, the fortress gradually lost its military significance. During this period, parts of the castle were converted into living quarters, and local residents began using sections of the structure for storage and trade.

During the 19th century, the castle fell into disrepair, with portions of the walls crumbling and vegetation taking over some of the abandoned areas. However, efforts to restore and preserve the castle began in the 20th century, leading to its current status as a historical monument and cultural site.

Today, Desenzano Castle is open to the public, allowing visitors to walk through its halls, climb its towers, and imagine what life was like in medieval times. Informational plaques placed throughout the site provide historical context, making it an educational experience as well as a visual spectacle.

## Getting There

Reaching the castle is simple, as it is located just a short walk from the town center. The path leading up to the entrance winds through charming old streets, offering glimpses of traditional Italian architecture along the way. Although the climb is slightly uphill, it is manageable for most visitors.

For those arriving by car, parking is available nearby, with a short walk required to reach the castle grounds. Public transportation options also connect Desenzano with other towns along Lake Garda, making it a convenient stop for travelers exploring the region.

## Things to Do at Desenzano Castle

**1. Enjoy the Panoramic Views:** The castle's elevated position provides one of the best viewpoints in Desenzano. Whether visiting during the clear skies of summer or the misty mornings of autumn, the views from the top are always impressive. The lake stretches out below, dotted with boats, while the red-tiled roofs of the town create a charming contrast against the blue water.

**2. Attend Cultural Events:** Throughout the year, the castle serves as a venue for various cultural activities. Concerts, theatrical performances, and seasonal festivals bring the site to life, offering visitors a chance to experience the castle in a dynamic setting.

**3. Explore the Historic Architecture:** Walking through the castle, visitors can appreciate the craftsmanship that went into its construction. The sturdy stone walls, arched passageways, and remnants of medieval rooms give a sense of the building's long history.

**4. Learn About the Local History:** For history enthusiasts, the castle provides insight into the defensive strategies of medieval Italy. Informational signs and guided tours offer details about the different phases of construction and the role the fortress played in Desenzano's development.

Desenzano Castle stands as a proud symbol of the town's past. With its well-preserved walls, fascinating history, and spectacular views, it is a must-visit for anyone exploring Lake Garda. The experience of walking through its ancient corridors and looking out over the lake makes it easy to see why this landmark has remained a cherished part of Desenzano for centuries.

## Roman Villa of Desenzano: A Peek into the Past

Tucked away near the shores of Lake Garda, the Roman Villa of Desenzano is one of northern Italy's most fascinating archaeological sites. As the largest and most well-preserved Roman villa in the region, it offers a rare glimpse into the opulence and daily life of the Roman elite. The villa's intricate mosaics, well-structured remains, and scenic location make it a must-visit for those interested in history, art, and ancient architecture.

## A Glimpse into Ancient Roman Luxury

The villa dates back to the late 1st century AD and was occupied for several centuries before falling into ruin. Archaeologists believe that it was a lavish lakeside retreat for a wealthy Roman noble or high-ranking official. During the height of the Roman Empire, Lake Garda was a favored location for aristocratic residences, thanks to its mild climate and beautiful surroundings.

Like many grand villas of the period, the residence was designed not only for comfort but also to impress. The layout suggests that it was meant to host elaborate gatherings, feasts, and entertainment. The presence of baths, courtyards, and decorative mosaics indicates that the villa was a place of relaxation and refinement, far removed from the political and commercial hustle of Rome.

## Architectural Highlights

Walking through the site today, visitors can see the foundations and partial walls of the villa, giving a sense of its original grandeur. Though time and the elements have worn away much of the structure, some of its most striking features remain intact.

**1. The Mosaic Floors:** The most captivating aspect of the villa is its series of remarkably well-preserved mosaics. These intricate artworks, made from thousands of tiny colored stones, depict scenes from mythology, nature, and daily Roman life. Among the most famous is a hunting scene that shows elegant figures chasing wild animals, demonstrating both the artistic skill and storytelling ability of Roman craftsmen.

Other mosaics feature geometric patterns and floral motifs, each showcasing a different aspect of Roman artistic expression. These floors would have been a sign of the owner's wealth and taste, as mosaic work was an expensive and highly regarded form of decoration in the ancient world.

**2. The Courtyards and Gardens:** The villa's design included multiple open courtyards and garden spaces, which would have been filled with lush greenery, fountains, and sculptures. These outdoor areas provided a peaceful retreat for the villa's residents and guests, allowing them to enjoy the lake's natural beauty while shaded by colonnades.

**3. The Baths and Heating System:** Like many luxurious Roman homes, the villa contained a private bath complex. Heated through an underground hypocaust system, these baths would have included hot, warm, and cold rooms, similar to a modern spa. Though only fragments of the original system remain, archaeologists have identified the layout of the bathing area and the channels that once carried hot air beneath the floors.

### The Rediscovery of the Villa

The ruins of the villa remained hidden for centuries, buried beneath layers of earth and debris. It wasn't until the 1920s that significant excavations began, revealing the true scale of the site. Archaeologists uncovered not just the floor plan of the villa but also countless artifacts, including pottery, tools, and decorative elements.

Since then, conservation efforts have been ongoing to protect the mosaics and preserve the remains for future generations. The site is now an open-air museum, with protective coverings and walkways allowing visitors to admire the mosaics and ruins without causing damage.

### Getting There

The Roman Villa of Desenzano is conveniently located near the town center, making it easily accessible on foot. A short walk from the main piazza and the lakefront brings visitors to the entrance, where tickets can be purchased for a self-guided or guided tour.

For those arriving by car, there are parking areas nearby. Public transportation also connects Desenzano with other towns around Lake Garda, allowing history enthusiasts to incorporate the villa into a broader itinerary of historical sites.

### Things to Do at the Roman Villa

**1. Admire the Mosaics Up Close:** Unlike many ancient sites where visitors are kept at a distance, the Roman Villa of Desenzano allows a surprisingly close view of its mosaic floors. Walkways guide guests over the ruins, providing the best angles to appreciate the detailed craftsmanship of these ancient works of art.

**2. Learn About Roman Daily Life:** Informational panels throughout the site explain the function of different rooms, offering insight into how the villa's residents lived, entertained, and relaxed. Guided tours, available at certain times of the year, provide a deeper understanding of the archaeological findings and the villa's historical significance.

**3. Enjoy the Scenic Location:** Standing on the villa's grounds, it's easy to understand why the Romans chose this spot for a luxurious retreat. The gentle breeze from the lake, the view of the rolling hills, and the peaceful surroundings create an atmosphere that still feels tranquil centuries later.

**4. Visit the On-Site Museum:** Adjacent to the villa, a small museum displays some of the artifacts uncovered during excavations. These include fragments of sculptures, tools, and everyday objects that give further context to the lives of those who once inhabited the villa.

The Roman Villa of Desenzano offers a rare and intimate look at the splendor of Roman life along Lake Garda. With its exceptional mosaics, architectural remains, and breathtaking setting, it stands as a testament to the region's rich history.

# Outdoor Activities and Relaxation

## Cycling and Walking Trails

Desenzano del Garda is an excellent destination for outdoor enthusiasts who enjoy walking and cycling. With its scenic lakefront, rolling hills, and historic town center, the area provides routes for all skill levels. From gentle strolls along the waterfront to more challenging cycling routes through the countryside, there are plenty of ways to enjoy the fresh air and beautiful landscapes.

**Walking Trails for Every Level**
Walking in Desenzano can be as relaxing or as challenging as you prefer. The town offers a mix of lakeside promenades, historic pathways, and countryside trails, allowing visitors to experience different aspects of the region on foot.

**1. Lakeside Promenade:** The lakeside promenade is a perfect route for those looking for a relaxing and scenic walk. Stretching along the shoreline, this path offers stunning views of the lake, with plenty of cafés and benches along the way. The promenade is flat and well-maintained, making it suitable for all ages. Morning and late afternoon walks are particularly pleasant, as the light reflects beautifully off the water.

**2. Historic Walk to Desenzano Castle:** For a walk that combines history and panoramic views, the route to Desenzano Castle is a great choice. Starting in the town center, this walk takes you through charming cobbled streets, past local shops and cafés, and gradually uphill to the castle. While the incline can be slightly challenging, the reward is a breathtaking view of Lake Garda from the top.

**3. Countryside and Vineyard Trails:** For those who want to step away from the town and experience the quieter side of Desenzano, several paths lead into the surrounding countryside. Walking through vineyards and olive groves provides a peaceful escape from the busier lakefront. The paths are well-marked, and depending on the route you choose, you may come across small local farms where you can stop for a wine tasting or a sampling of fresh produce.

**4. Trail to Lonato del Garda:** A longer but rewarding walk leads from Desenzano to Lonato del Garda, a nearby town known for its medieval architecture. This route is approximately 5 km and takes walkers through rolling countryside, offering scenic views of Lake Garda along the way. Once in Lonato, visitors can explore the Rocca di Lonato, a historic fortress with panoramic views of the region.

**Cycling Routes for All Skill Levels**

Desenzano del Garda is an excellent starting point for cycling adventures. The town has several bike rental shops that offer traditional bikes and e-bikes for those who prefer some assistance on steeper climbs. Routes range from flat, relaxed rides along the lake to more intense hill climbs in the Morainic Hills.

**Easy Route: Desenzano to Sirmione (10 km)**

This route follows a mostly flat path along the southern shore of Lake Garda, making it ideal for beginners. The ride offers stunning lake views and passes through charming residential areas. Sirmione, famous for its Scaliger Castle and thermal baths, is a perfect destination for a break before returning to Desenzano.

### Moderate Route: Vineyard and Countryside Loop (25 km)
For those looking for a slightly more challenging ride, a loop through the countryside surrounding Desenzano offers a mix of paved and gravel roads. This route takes cyclists through vineyards and small villages such as Pozzolengo, where you can stop for a wine tasting or a traditional meal. The rolling terrain provides a good workout without being too strenuous.

### Challenging Route: Morainic Hills and Castellaro Lagusello (50 km)
For experienced cyclists looking for a challenge, the Morainic Hills provide an excellent opportunity for a more intense ride. This route takes riders through undulating terrain with a few steep climbs. The ride to Castellaro Lagusello, a small medieval village, is particularly rewarding. Once there, cyclists can take a break and explore the well-preserved historic center before heading back to Desenzano.

### Tips for Enjoying the Trails
➡ Wear comfortable footwear: Whether walking or cycling, good shoes make a big difference.

➡ Stay hydrated: Carry water, especially during summer, as shaded areas can be limited.

➡ Start early or late in the day: Mornings and evenings are cooler and less crowded.

➡ Use an e-bike if needed: The rolling hills can be challenging, and an e-bike allows for a more enjoyable ride.

➡ Follow marked trails: Most routes are well-signposted, but it's always helpful to have a map or a GPS device.

With its scenic routes, historic landmarks, and opportunities to experience the countryside, Desenzano del Garda provides the perfect setting for walking and cycling.

## Water Activities and Leisure

Desenzano del Garda, with its prime location on the southern shores of Lake Garda, offers a range of water-based activities and leisure options for visitors seeking both adventure and relaxation. The town's marinas, beaches, and clear waters make it an ideal destination for swimming, sailing, kayaking, paddleboarding, and boat tours. If you're looking for a peaceful afternoon by the lake or an active day on the water, Desenzano provides plenty of opportunities to enjoy the lake from different perspectives.

**Swimming and Sunbathing**
Desenzano del Garda has several well-maintained beaches where visitors can swim, relax, and enjoy the sunshine. The town's shoreline features a mix of sandy and pebble beaches, with calm waters that make swimming pleasant and safe.

- **Desenzanino Beach**: Located just a short walk from the town center, this beach is one of the most popular spots for sunbathing and swimming. It features sunbeds and umbrellas for rent, as well as nearby cafés and restaurants for refreshments. The water is shallow near the shore, making it suitable for families with children.
- **Spiaggia d'Oro (Golden Beach)**: Situated slightly further from the town center, this beach has a more relaxed atmosphere and offers a mix of sand and pebbles. It's a great spot to spend a few hours unwinding, with clear water and a beautiful view of the lake.
- **Porto Rivoltella**: In the Rivoltella district of Desenzano, this lakeside area has a peaceful beach with grassy areas for those who prefer not to sit on pebbles. There's also a lakeside promenade, perfect for a scenic walk after a swim.

The best time to enjoy the beaches is in the morning or late afternoon when the sun is not too intense, and the crowds are smaller. While some areas are free, others have private beach clubs where visitors can rent loungers and access additional services.

## Sailing and Boat Rentals

Lake Garda's steady winds and open waters make it a fantastic location for sailing. Visitors who want to experience the lake from a different perspective can rent a sailboat or take part in a sailing tour.

➪ **Sailing Schools and Lessons**: Several local sailing schools offer courses for beginners, as well as rentals for experienced sailors. Whether you're looking for a private lesson or a group experience, professional instructors are available to guide you through the basics.

➪ **Boat Rentals**: For those who prefer a more private experience, motorboats and small sailboats can be rented from the town's marina. Some boats require a license, but there are also options for those who don't have one. Renting a boat allows visitors to explore hidden coves, swim in secluded areas, and enjoy the lake at their own pace.

➪ **Guided Sailing Excursions**: If you'd rather leave the navigation to an expert, joining a sailing tour is a great way to relax on the water while taking in views of the surrounding mountains and picturesque lakeside villages. Some tours include stops for swimming or aperitivo on board.

## Kayaking and Stand-Up Paddleboarding

For a more active way to enjoy the lake, kayaking and stand-up paddleboarding (SUP) are excellent choices. These activities allow visitors to explore the coastline up close while getting a great workout.

➪ **Kayaking**: Renting a kayak is an easy and enjoyable way to move along the shoreline, discovering quiet bays and scenic spots. Single and double kayaks are available at various rental locations, with some companies also offering guided excursions. Paddling along the lake in the early morning, when the water is calm and the surroundings are peaceful, is particularly rewarding.

➪ **Stand-Up Paddleboarding (SUP)**: Stand-up paddleboarding has become increasingly popular on Lake Garda, thanks to its smooth waters and beautiful scenery. Beginners can take lessons, while more experienced paddleboarders can rent equipment and set off on their own. SUP is a great way to connect with nature while enjoying the lake's tranquil atmosphere.

## Water Sports and Adventure Activities

For visitors looking for more excitement, Desenzano del Garda offers several high-energy water activities.

⇨ **Wakeboarding and Water Skiing**: Several local operators provide wakeboarding and water skiing experiences for both beginners and experienced riders. These activities offer an adrenaline rush while allowing participants to take in the stunning backdrop of the lake.

⇨ **Windsurfing and Kitesurfing**: While northern Lake Garda is more famous for strong winds, Desenzano's steady breezes still make it a good location for windsurfing and kitesurfing. Equipment rentals and lessons are available for those who want to try these exhilarating sports.

⇨ **Jet Skiing**: For those who want to speed across the water, jet ski rentals are available at various points along the lake. Some operators offer guided jet ski tours that take riders to different areas of Lake Garda.

## Boat Tours and Lake Cruises

A boat tour is a perfect way to appreciate Lake Garda's vastness and beauty while learning more about its history and geography. Several types of tours are available, ranging from short sightseeing cruises to full-day excursions.

⇨ **Short Scenic Cruises**: Many operators offer one- or two-hour cruises departing from Desenzano's harbor. These tours typically pass by nearby towns like Sirmione, where visitors can admire its castle and Roman ruins from the water.

⇨ **Full-Day Excursions**: For a more immersive experience, full-day boat tours take passengers to multiple destinations around the lake. These excursions often include stops in picturesque villages such as Limone sul Garda and Malcesine, with free time to explore each location. Some tours provide onboard meals or aperitivo.

⇨ **Sunset and Private Cruises**: For a more romantic experience, sunset cruises allow guests to enjoy the changing colors of the lake while sipping local wine. Private boat charters are also available for those who want a more personalized trip.

**Relaxing by the Marina and Waterfront**

For visitors who prefer to stay on dry land while still enjoying the lake, Desenzano's waterfront is a great place to unwind. The town's marina is a lively area with cafés, gelaterias, and restaurants offering lakeside dining. Watching boats come and go while enjoying an espresso or an aperitivo is a perfect way to soak in the relaxed atmosphere.

Several parks and green spaces along the lake also provide a quiet place to sit and enjoy the view. The promenade connecting the beaches and town center is ideal for a leisurely walk, especially in the evening when the lights reflect off the water.

Lake Garda's waters offer something for everyone, from active sports enthusiasts to those seeking tranquility. Whether swimming in the clear waters, paddling along the shore, or setting sail on an afternoon cruise, Desenzano provides plenty of ways to enjoy the beauty of the lake.

# CHAPTER 7: LIMONE SUL GARDA – A PICTURESQUE GETAWAY

## Exploring the Old Town and Historic Sites

Limone sul Garda, a charming town on the northwestern shore of Lake Garda, offers a mix of history, natural beauty, and traditional Italian character. Despite its name, which suggests a connection to lemons, Limone's origins are not linked to citrus but rather to the Latin word limes, meaning border. Once an isolated fishing village, it has grown into a destination known for its historic sites, narrow streets, and cultural heritage.

Walking through the old town is like stepping into the past. The streets are lined with pastel-colored houses, wrought-iron balconies, and archways that have stood for centuries. The lakefront promenade provides a perfect starting point, offering stunning views before leading visitors into the heart of the historic district. Small boutiques, artisan shops, and traditional cafés add to the town's character, making it an ideal place to wander and soak in the atmosphere.

The history of Limone is deeply tied to its landscape. For centuries, its residents relied on fishing, olive cultivation, and citrus farming. The town's isolation, due to the steep mountains that rise behind it, meant that it remained relatively untouched by major developments until the mid-20th century. The construction of the Gardesana Occidentale road in 1932 changed everything, connecting Limone to other lakeside towns and bringing in visitors eager to experience its charm.

Among the town's most notable historical sites are the ancient lemon groves, which tell the story of a time when citrus farming was at the heart of Limone's economy. These groves, along with the centuries-old San Benedetto Church, provide insight into the town's heritage and the resilience of its people.

## The Ancient Lemon Groves of Limone

The lemon groves of Limone sul Garda are a defining feature of this lakeside town, reflecting a long history of ingenuity and agricultural adaptation. While Lake Garda's northern location might seem unsuitable for citrus cultivation, Limone's unique microclimate—shielded by mountains and warmed by the lake's waters—has allowed lemon trees to thrive for centuries. These groves, known as *limonaie*, are not just agricultural plots but historical landmarks that showcase the town's deep-rooted connection to citrus farming.

The structured cultivation of lemons in Limone dates back to the 17th century when Franciscan monks introduced innovative methods to protect trees from cold winters. They built terraced gardens on the steep slopes surrounding the town, constructing tall stone walls and wooden frameworks that could be covered with glass panels or cloth during colder months. This technique allowed farmers to grow lemons, oranges, and other citrus fruits in conditions far from their usual Mediterranean habitat.

At its peak, the lemon industry played a major role in Limone's economy. By the 18th and 19th centuries, the town had become one of the northernmost locations in Europe where citrus fruits were grown commercially. Lemons from Limone were highly valued and exported across Italy and even to parts of Central Europe. Their essential oils were used in perfumes, their peels in liqueurs, and their juice in medicinal remedies. The town's economy flourished, with families dedicating their lives to citrus farming and trade.

However, this golden era of lemon cultivation eventually declined. By the early 20th century, advances in transportation and refrigeration made it easier to import citrus fruits from southern Italy, where growing conditions were naturally more favorable. At the same time, the high costs of maintaining the traditional *limonaie* became unsustainable. Many lemon groves were abandoned, and Limone's agricultural focus shifted toward olive cultivation and tourism.

Today, the legacy of Limone's citrus heritage is carefully preserved, and one of the best places to experience it is **Limonaia del Castel**. This restored lemon house, located in the heart of the old town, offers visitors an insight into the history and techniques of traditional lemon farming. Walking through its terraced gardens, you can see rows of citrus trees supported by stone pillars and wooden beams, just as they were centuries ago. Informative displays explain the growing process, from planting to harvest, and highlight the methods used to protect the trees during the winter months.

Beyond Limonaia del Castel, remnants of other historic lemon groves can still be seen scattered throughout the town, integrated into gardens, pathways, and private properties. These sites serve as reminders of the town's agricultural past and its adaptation to the rugged terrain of Lake Garda's shores.

Lemon culture remains deeply woven into Limone's identity. Many local businesses produce and sell citrus-based goods, from **limoncello**, a traditional Italian lemon liqueur, to lemon-infused olive oils, jams, and scented soaps. Restaurants in Limone often incorporate lemons into their dishes, using the bright citrus flavor to enhance everything from freshly caught lake fish to refreshing sorbets.

The town also celebrates its citrus heritage with festivals and seasonal markets featuring lemon-themed decorations, food, and artisan products. These events bring locals and visitors together, keeping the tradition alive and reinforcing Limone's reputation as a place where history, culture, and nature intertwine.

The ancient lemon groves of Limone are more than just an agricultural relic—they are a testament to human perseverance and creativity. They represent a time when Limone was an essential part of Italy's citrus trade and continue to be a source of pride for the community. Walking among these terraced gardens, with their fragrant blossoms and sun-ripened fruit, provides a sense of connection to the past and a deeper appreciation for the traditions that shaped this remarkable town.

## San Benedetto Church: A Symbol of History

San Benedetto Church stands as one of the most significant landmarks in Limone sul Garda, offering a blend of history, architectural beauty, and a peaceful atmosphere. Situated in the heart of the town, this centuries-old church has been a spiritual and cultural center for generations of Limone's residents. Whether you are drawn to historical sites, religious landmarks, or simply looking for a quiet place to reflect, San Benedetto provides a meaningful experience.

**A Look at the History**
San Benedetto Church, also known as **Chiesa di San Benedetto**, dates back to the 11th century, though much of its current structure was developed in later centuries. The church was originally built in a simple Romanesque style, but over time, renovations and expansions introduced Baroque influences, giving it the ornate interior seen today. The Benedictine monks who once lived in the region played a key role in shaping the church's religious and cultural significance.

During the 17th and 18th centuries, San Benedetto underwent major refurbishments, including the addition of decorative frescoes, intricate stucco work, and an elegant bell tower that now defines Limone's skyline. Over the years, the church has served as a place of worship, a refuge during times of hardship, and a gathering point for local religious festivals and ceremonies.

**Architectural Highlights**
From the outside, San Benedetto's façade is simple yet charming, featuring a pale stone exterior that blends harmoniously with the

surrounding town. The bell tower rises above the rooftops, offering a picturesque contrast against the backdrop of Lake Garda and the towering mountains.

Stepping inside, visitors are greeted by a richly decorated interior. The high, arched ceilings are adorned with delicate frescoes that depict biblical scenes, while intricate stucco embellishments add depth to the walls and ceiling. The church's Baroque altar is particularly striking, featuring gilded details and religious artwork that capture the devotion and artistic craftsmanship of the era.

A highlight for many visitors is the **organ loft**, where an impressive 18th-century pipe organ still stands. If you visit during a religious service or a special event, you may have the opportunity to hear it in action, filling the church with deep, resonant tones that enhance the serene atmosphere.

## What to Do There

San Benedetto Church offers more than just historical and architectural significance. Here are a few ways to make the most of your visit:

➪ **Admire the Frescoes and Artwork:** Take time to appreciate the beautiful frescoes and altar decorations that tell stories from the Bible. The artwork, created by local and regional painters, reflects centuries of devotion and artistic evolution.

➪ **Attend a Church Service:** If you are interested in experiencing local traditions, consider attending a Mass. Services are held regularly, and even if you do not understand Italian, the experience of sitting among locals in a centuries-old church can be meaningful.

➪ **Enjoy the Peaceful Atmosphere:** The church provides a quiet escape from the more crowded areas of Limone. Whether you are religious or not, the tranquil setting makes it a perfect place to sit, reflect, or simply enjoy a moment of calm.

➪ **Explore the Surrounding Area:** San Benedetto is located near the historic center of Limone, making it easy to combine your visit with a stroll through the town's charming streets. After visiting the church, consider stopping at a nearby café, walking down to the lakeside promenade, or exploring local artisan shops.

**How to Get There**

San Benedetto Church is conveniently located in Limone sul Garda's old town, making it easy to reach on foot from most parts of the village.

🚶 **By Foot:** The church is a short walk from the town center. Simply follow the cobbled streets uphill, and you'll arrive at the church in about five to ten minutes. Signs throughout Limone help guide visitors to key landmarks, including San Benedetto.

🚗 **By Car:** If you are coming from another town along Lake Garda, you can drive to Limone and park in one of the designated public parking areas. The closest parking lot is near the town center, from which you can walk up to the church in a few minutes.

⛴ **By Boat:** Many visitors arrive in Limone by ferry from other towns around Lake Garda, such as Riva del Garda, Malcesine, or Desenzano. From the ferry terminal, it's a pleasant ten-minute walk through the town to reach the church.

San Benedetto Church is more than just a place of worship; it is a living testament to Limone's rich history and a peaceful retreat where visitors can appreciate both spiritual and artistic beauty.

# High-End Stays and Fine Dining

## Best Luxury Hotels

Limone sul Garda has a selection of high-end hotels that provide premium comfort, excellent service, and breathtaking views of Lake Garda. Below are six top luxury hotels, each offering a unique experience.

### 1. EALA – My Lakeside Dream

🏠 **Address:** Via IV Novembre, 86, 25010 Limone sul Garda, Italy

📍 **GPS Coordinates:** 45.8061° N, 10.7914° E

💲 **Pricing:** From €450 per night

🏛 **Amenities:**

➡ Infinity pool with panoramic lake views

➡ Private beach access

⇨ Full-service spa with sauna and Turkish bath
⇨ Gourmet restaurant with tasting menus
⇨ Modern suites with private balconies

EALA is an adults-only resort designed for travelers seeking peace, wellness, and top-tier hospitality. The sleek, modern design blends with the natural surroundings, creating a relaxing retreat.

## 2. Park Hotel Imperial

🏠 **Address:** Via Tamas, 10/B, 25010 Limone sul Garda, Italy

📍 **GPS Coordinates:** 45.8107° N, 10.7923° E

💲 **Pricing:** From €300 per night

🏛 **Amenities:**

⇨ Outdoor and indoor swimming pools
⇨ Spa with Turkish bath, saltwater pool, and massages
⇨ Tennis courts and fitness center
⇨ Fine dining restaurant
⇨ Rooms with private balconies

Park Hotel Imperial offers a mix of classic elegance and modern comfort. Its wellness center is a major draw for guests looking to unwind with thermal treatments.

## 3. Hotel Splendid Palace

🏠 **Address:** Via IV Novembre, 70, 25010 Limone sul Garda, Italy

📍 **GPS Coordinates:** 45.8073° N, 10.7918° E

💲 **Pricing:** From €220 per night

🏛 **Amenities:**

⇨ Two swimming pools (indoor and outdoor)
⇨ Rooftop terrace with lake views
⇨ All-inclusive dining options
⇨ Private garden with sun loungers
⇨ Rooms with lake-view balconies

Located near the historic center, Hotel Splendid Palace is ideal for guests who want convenience, stunning scenery, and a relaxing atmosphere.

### 4. Hotel Monte Baldo
🏠 **Address:** Via Porto, 29, 25010 Limone sul Garda, Italy
📍 **GPS Coordinates:** 45.8112° N, 10.7940° E
💲 **Pricing:** From €180 per night
🏨 **Amenities:**
⇨ Lakefront location with private dock
⇨ Boutique-style design
⇨ Traditional Italian restaurant with terrace seating
⇨ Rooms with rustic-chic décor
⇨ Warm, family-run hospitality

For travelers who prefer a charming and intimate experience, Hotel Monte Baldo provides a cozy setting with personalized service.

### 5. Hotel Alexander
🏠 **Address:** Lungolago Marconi, 58, 25010 Limone sul Garda, Italy
📍 **GPS Coordinates:** 45.8119° N, 10.7949° E
💲 **Pricing:** From €250 per night
🏨 **Amenities:**
⇨ Outdoor pool with sun terrace
⇨ Wellness center with sauna and Jacuzzi
⇨ Restaurant serving Mediterranean cuisine
⇨ Spacious rooms with modern décor
⇨ Close proximity to the lakeside promenade

This hotel is a perfect option for those who want a balance of relaxation and easy access to Limone's waterfront.

### 6. Hotel Capo Reamol
🏠 **Address:** Via IV Novembre, 92, 25010 Limone sul Garda, Italy
📍 **GPS Coordinates:** 45.8045° N, 10.7903° E
💲 **Pricing:** From €200 per night
🏨 **Amenities:**
⇨ Private beach with sun loungers
⇨ Windsurfing and sailing school
⇨ Outdoor swimming pool
⇨ Restaurant with terrace seating

⇨ Rooms with direct lake views

Hotel Capo Reamol is a great choice for travelers who love water sports or simply want a secluded lakeside retreat.

## Fine Dining with a View

Limone sul Garda has several excellent restaurants that combine high-quality cuisine with breathtaking lake views. Here are six of the best options.

### 1. La Cantina del Baffo

🏠 **Address:** Via Mons. Daniele Comboni, 33, 25010 Limone sul Garda, Italy

📍 **GPS Coordinates:** 45.8116° N, 10.7947° E

This restaurant is known for its refined Italian dishes and carefully curated wine list. The cozy, intimate setting makes it perfect for a relaxed evening meal. The pasta dishes, fresh seafood, and locally sourced ingredients highlight the flavors of the region.

### 2. Ristorante Gemma

🏠 **Address:** Via Porto, 26, 25010 Limone sul Garda, Italy

📍 **GPS Coordinates:** 45.8113° N, 10.7942° E

Ristorante Gemma offers fresh seafood and traditional Italian dishes right on the lakefront. The outdoor terrace provides an incredible dining experience, with the water just a few steps away. The risotto and grilled lake fish are standout menu items.

### 3. Al Vecchio Fontec

🏠 **Address:** Via Castello, 2, 25010 Limone sul Garda, Italy

📍 **GPS Coordinates:** 45.8120° N, 10.7941° E

Located near Limone's historic castle, Al Vecchio Fontec serves homemade pasta, premium meats, and an excellent selection of wines. The terrace provides stunning views of the town and lake, making it a great spot for a leisurely meal.

### 4. Ristorante Monte Baldo

🏠 **Address:** Via Porto, 29, 25010 Limone sul Garda, Italy

**GPS Coordinates:** 45.8112° N, 10.7940° E

This restaurant is part of Hotel Monte Baldo and offers fine Italian cuisine with a focus on fresh, seasonal ingredients. Guests can dine on the terrace while enjoying a peaceful lakeside atmosphere. The homemade pasta and fresh fish dishes are highly recommended.

### 5. Osteria Da Livio

**Address:** Via Tamas, 17, 25010 Limone sul Garda, Italy

**GPS Coordinates:** 45.8125° N, 10.7920° E

Osteria Da Livio is a bit further from the main tourist area but offers a unique dining experience in a more rustic setting. The menu features high-quality meats, house-made pasta, and a strong selection of regional wines. The cozy interior and welcoming service make it a great choice for a relaxed evening.

### 6. Ristorante Al Pirata

**Address:** Via Lungolago Guglielmo Marconi, 36, 25010 Limone sul Garda, Italy

**GPS Coordinates:** 45.8109° N, 10.7945° E

Al Pirata provides lakeside dining with an extensive seafood menu. The atmosphere is elegant yet relaxed, and the restaurant prides itself on using the freshest ingredients. The grilled lake fish and seafood risotto are standout choices.

Fine dining in Limone sul Garda typically ranges from **€40 to €100 per person**, with many restaurants offering wine pairings and multi-course meals. To secure a table with the best view, reservations are recommended, especially during peak tourist season. Most establishments offer outdoor seating, allowing guests to enjoy their meals while overlooking the beautiful lake and surrounding mountains.

# Waterside Relaxation & Outdoor Fun

## Beautiful Beaches for Swimming

Limone sul Garda is home to some of the most scenic beaches along Lake Garda's northern shores. Unlike the sandy beaches found in some other parts of Italy, Limone's beaches are primarily pebbled, with crystal-clear water and breathtaking mountain views. The town's position along the lake's western shore provides a mix of both popular and secluded beaches, making it a great destination for swimming and lakeside relaxation.

**Spiaggia Tifu: A Popular Choice for Swimming**

Spiaggia Tifu is one of the most well-known beaches in Limone sul Garda. Located just a short walk from the town center, this beach offers a comfortable setting for swimmers of all levels. The smooth pebbles make entering the water easy, and the lake floor slopes gently, allowing for a safe swimming experience. The water here is exceptionally clear, with visibility extending several meters below the surface.

The beach is equipped with sun loungers and umbrellas for rent, making it a convenient place to spend a few hours or an entire day. There are also showers and changing rooms available, adding to the comfort of visitors. A small café nearby offers cold drinks, snacks, and fresh gelato, making it easy to grab refreshments without having to leave the waterfront.

Since Spiaggia Tifu is one of the more popular beaches in Limone, it tends to get busy during the summer months. Arriving early in the day is the best way to secure a good spot, especially on weekends when both tourists and locals gather here.

**Spiaggia Grostol: A Hidden Gem for Peaceful Swimming**

For those looking for a quieter beach, Spiaggia Grostol provides a more secluded option. This beach is located slightly south of the main town area and is often overlooked by visitors, making it a great place for those who prefer a peaceful setting. The entrance to the water is slightly rockier than Spiaggia Tifu, so wearing water shoes can be helpful. However, the lack of large crowds and the clear, undisturbed water make up for it.

The swimming conditions here are excellent, with deeper waters a short distance from the shore. This makes it an ideal spot for more experienced swimmers who want to enjoy a longer swim without interruption. The surrounding landscape, with towering cliffs and lush greenery, adds to the natural beauty of the setting.

There are no official facilities at Spiaggia Grostol, so bringing water and snacks is recommended. The beach is accessible by foot or bicycle, with a small parking area nearby for those arriving by car.

## Cola Beach: A Family-Friendly Spot

Cola Beach is a great option for families with children. The gentle slope of the lakebed ensures that the shallow waters near the shore are safe for kids, while adults can swim further out into the deeper areas. The beach also has a grassy section where families can set up picnic blankets and enjoy a meal by the water.

In addition to swimming, Cola Beach has a small playground and a volleyball court, making it a fun location for children and teenagers. The nearby promenade is lined with restaurants and cafés, providing easy access to meals and refreshments.

Sun loungers and umbrellas are available for rent, and there are also public restrooms and changing facilities. The relaxed atmosphere and range of amenities make this beach a favorite among visitors looking for a convenient and enjoyable spot to spend the day.

## Fonte Torrente San Giovanni Beach: Scenic Views and Pristine Waters

One of the most picturesque beaches in Limone sul Garda, Fonte Torrente San Giovanni Beach is known for its exceptionally clean water and stunning mountain backdrop. This beach is located near the mouth of a small stream that flows into the lake, creating a unique natural setting.

The beach itself is made up of small pebbles, and the water is incredibly clear, making it a great place for snorkeling as well as swimming. The transition from shallow to deep water is gradual, so it accommodates both beginners and stronger swimmers.

Fonte Torrente San Giovanni Beach is less commercialized than some of the larger beaches, meaning there are fewer facilities, but this also helps maintain its peaceful charm. Visitors often bring their own beach towels and picnic supplies to enjoy a relaxed day by the water.

## Tips for Enjoying the Beaches in Limone sul Garda

➡ Arrive early: The beaches in Limone can become busy, especially in peak summer months. Arriving in the morning ensures a good spot and a more peaceful experience.

➡ Wear water shoes: Most of the beaches in Limone are pebbled, which can be uncomfortable for sensitive feet. Water shoes make it easier to enter and exit the lake.

➡ Bring sunscreen and shade: While some beaches offer sun umbrellas for rent, others have little to no natural shade. A hat, sunscreen, and a beach umbrella can help protect against the sun.

➡ Pack a picnic: Some of the more secluded beaches don't have cafés or restaurants nearby, so bringing snacks and drinks is a good idea.

➡ Check the weather: Lake Garda is generally calm, but occasional winds can create choppy waters. Checking the forecast before heading out ensures a safer and more enjoyable swim.

## How to Get to the Beaches

Most of the beaches in Limone sul Garda are easily accessible by foot from the town center. A scenic lakeside promenade connects several of the main beaches, allowing visitors to walk or cycle between them. For those driving, parking is available near Spiaggia Tifu and Cola Beach, though spaces can fill up quickly in the summer. Public transportation, including local buses, also connects Limone sul Garda with nearby towns, providing another way to reach the beaches.

Boat services operate between different areas of Lake Garda, making it possible to visit beaches in Limone as part of a day trip from towns such as Riva del Garda or Malcesine. Taking a ferry offers a unique perspective of the lake and allows for a stress-free way to reach the best swimming spots in the area.

## Boating and Kayaking on the Lake

Limone sul Garda is one of the most scenic locations for boating and kayaking on Lake Garda. The dramatic cliffs rising from the water, the picturesque town along the shoreline, and the vast expanse of the lake make it an excellent setting for those who want to spend time on the water. With options ranging from guided tours to self-rented boats, visitors of all experience levels can find a way to enjoy the lake at their own pace.

**Kayaking Along Limone sul Garda's Shoreline**
Kayaking is one of the most enjoyable ways to experience Lake Garda up close. The calm, clear waters make for a smooth ride, while the rugged cliffs and lush greenery provide a beautiful backdrop. Kayaking allows access to areas that boats cannot reach, such as small inlets, secluded beaches, and caves along the lake's edge.
One of the most rewarding routes starts from Limone's main harbor and follows the shoreline toward the north. Paddlers will pass by lemon groves, rocky cliffs, and small beaches where they can stop for a break. A popular destination for kayakers is the area near the Grotte di Mezzema, a set of caves that are best reached by water. The stillness of a kayak allows for a quiet approach, making it possible to see fish and other aquatic life in the lake's crystal-clear waters.
Kayak rentals are available at several spots along the waterfront, with options for both solo and tandem kayaks. For those new to kayaking, guided tours are a good choice, as they offer instruction and insights into the history and geography of the area.

**Boat Rentals for a Private Experience**
For visitors who want to explore the lake at their own pace, renting a boat is an excellent option. Rental companies in Limone offer a variety of boats, including motorboats that do not require a boating license. These are perfect for families or small groups who want the freedom to explore different areas of the lake.
With a rented boat, visitors can head south toward the town of Gargnano or cross the lake to Malcesine, known for its medieval castle. Another option is to venture north toward Riva del Garda, where the lake narrows and the mountains become even more dramatic.

Most boat rentals include fuel, safety equipment, and a brief instruction session on how to operate the boat. Rental durations typically range from one hour to a full day, giving plenty of flexibility for those who want either a quick outing or a long day on the water.

## Sailing Adventures on Lake Garda

Lake Garda is known for its excellent sailing conditions, particularly in the afternoon when the famous "Ora" wind picks up. This steady breeze creates ideal conditions for sailing, and Limone sul Garda has several options for both experienced sailors and those looking to learn. Several sailing schools in the area offer lessons and boat rentals, including small sailboats for independent use. Visitors with previous sailing experience can rent a boat for a few hours or an entire day, while those new to sailing can join a group lesson or take a private class with an instructor.

For a more relaxed experience, sailing tours provide a way to enjoy the lake without the need for any prior experience. These tours range from short excursions around Limone to longer trips that include stops in other towns along the lake. Some sailing charters even offer sunset cruises, which provide a stunning view of the sun setting behind the mountains.

## Paddleboarding for a Unique Perspective

For those looking for a mix of balance and adventure, stand-up paddleboarding (SUP) is another way to enjoy the lake. Paddleboarding offers a different perspective from both kayaking and boating, allowing for a full-body workout while gliding across the water.

The calm morning hours are the best time for paddleboarding, as the lake is usually smooth and there are fewer boats. Many of the same rental shops that offer kayaks also provide paddleboards, making it easy to try out this activity.

Paddleboarding is especially enjoyable along Limone's shoreline, where the water is clear enough to see fish swimming below. Some paddleboarders even take their boards to small beaches or rocky outcrops where they can rest before continuing on their route.

**Fishing on Lake Garda**

Lake Garda is home to a variety of fish species, making it a good spot for fishing. While shore fishing is common, renting a small boat allows anglers to reach deeper waters where fish such as pike, perch, and trout can be found.

Fishing permits are required, and they can be obtained from local fishing shops or online. Some boat rental companies offer fishing-specific rentals, complete with equipment and guidance on the best fishing spots around Limone.

**Tips for Enjoying Boating and Kayaking on Lake Garda**

➡ Check the weather forecast: The lake is generally calm in the morning, but winds can pick up in the afternoon. It's best to plan outings early in the day for the smoothest conditions.

➡ Wear proper gear: A life jacket is essential for safety, and water shoes can be helpful for getting in and out of kayaks.

➡ Respect local regulations: Certain areas of the lake have speed limits or restrictions on motorized boats. Be sure to follow any posted guidelines.

➡ Stay hydrated and wear sun protection: The sun can be strong, especially on the open water. Bringing water, sunscreen, and a hat will help prevent dehydration and sunburn.

➡ Book rentals in advance: During the summer months, boats and kayaks can be in high demand. Booking ahead ensures availability and avoids long wait times.

**How to Get to the Boating and Kayaking Areas**

Most rental shops and tour operators are located along Limone sul Garda's waterfront, close to the main harbor. The town is easily accessible by car, and there are parking areas nearby. For visitors staying in other parts of Lake Garda, ferries connect Limone with towns such as Malcesine and Riva del Garda, making it possible to visit for a day of water activities.

Boating and kayaking provide some of the best ways to experience Lake Garda from a new perspective. Whether paddling along the shoreline, sailing with the wind, or enjoying the freedom of a motorboat, the lake's natural beauty and calm waters make it a perfect setting for an outdoor adventure.

# CHAPTER 8: HIDDEN TREASURES OF LAKE GARDA

## Discovering Off-the-Beaten-Path Destinations

Lake Garda is well known for its famous towns and bustling lakeside promenades, but beyond the usual tourist spots, there are lesser-known locations that offer just as much charm and beauty. These places provide a different experience—one of quiet streets, historic buildings, and landscapes that feel untouched by crowds. Exploring these hidden treasures allows visitors to appreciate the lake's diverse character, from sleepy fishing villages to panoramic viewpoints that remain largely undiscovered.

### Quaint Villages with Unique Charm

Lake Garda is home to several small villages that have retained their historic character while offering a peaceful escape from the busier towns along the lake. These villages are perfect for those who appreciate a slower pace, traditional architecture, and a deep sense of local culture. Many of them are nestled in the hills, surrounded by olive groves and vineyards, while others sit right by the water with small harbors and quiet promenades. Here are some of the most charming villages to visit.

## Cassone di Malcesine

Cassone is a tiny fishing village just a few kilometers south of Malcesine. It is best known for the Aril River, one of the shortest rivers in the world at only 175 meters in length. The river flows through the village before reaching the lake, creating a picturesque setting with small bridges and traditional houses lining its banks.

The village itself has a relaxed atmosphere, with narrow streets and a small harbor where local fishermen still bring in their daily catch. Along the waterfront, visitors can find a few family-run trattorias serving fresh lake fish, homemade pasta, and regional wines. The views from Cassone are stunning, especially at sunset when the lake reflects the changing colors of the sky.

For those interested in history, Cassone has a small but fascinating museum dedicated to fishing and the life of past generations. Walking through the village feels like stepping back in time, as much of the original architecture has been preserved, and there is little modern development.

## Campo di Brenzone

Campo is an abandoned medieval village hidden in the hills above Brenzone sul Garda. It can only be reached by foot, making it one of the most secluded and peaceful spots on Lake Garda. The village consists of old stone houses, some in ruins, while others have been carefully maintained.

The Church of San Pietro in Vincoli is one of the village's most notable landmarks. This small Romanesque chapel dates back to the 13th century and features faded frescoes on its walls. Despite its age, the church remains in good condition and is still occasionally used for services.

Reaching Campo requires a short but scenic hike, winding through olive groves and offering glimpses of the lake below. The lack of roads and modern infrastructure makes it feel like a forgotten corner of history. It is an ideal place for those who enjoy quiet walks and the beauty of an untouched landscape.

## Canale di Tenno

Canale di Tenno is a medieval village located in the hills above Riva del Garda. It is one of the best-preserved historic villages in the region, with narrow cobbled alleys, stone archways, and rustic houses that have changed little over the centuries.

One of the most special times to visit Canale is during the artisan market held in December. The village transforms into a festive scene with stalls selling handmade crafts, traditional food, and mulled wine. In summer, an arts festival brings painters, musicians, and sculptors to the village, continuing a long tradition of artistic expression.

A short walk from Canale leads to Lago di Tenno, a small turquoise lake known for its striking color. The lake is surrounded by forests and offers an excellent spot for a quiet swim or a picnic. The combination of Canale's medieval charm and the natural beauty of Lago di Tenno makes this area a perfect destination for those seeking a peaceful retreat.

## Pieve di Tremosine

Pieve is a small village perched on the cliffs of the western shore of Lake Garda. The village is part of the larger Tremosine municipality, which consists of several scattered hamlets connected by winding mountain roads. Pieve itself is best known for its dramatic views and well-preserved historic center.

One of the most famous spots in Pieve is the Terrazza del Brivido, a viewing platform that extends over the edge of the cliff. From here, visitors can look down at the lake far below, with the mountains rising in the background. It is one of the most breathtaking views on Lake Garda and a favorite stop for photographers.

Pieve is also home to a number of traditional restaurants that serve local specialties, including polenta dishes and fresh cheeses produced in the nearby mountains. Walking through the village's narrow streets, visitors will find small chapels, stone houses, and hidden courtyards that give the place an old-world charm.

For those who enjoy scenic drives, the Strada della Forra passes near Pieve. This winding road, carved into the cliffs, was famously described by Winston Churchill as the eighth wonder of the world. It is an exciting route that offers dramatic views at every turn.

## Tignale

Tignale is a collection of small hamlets spread across the hills above the lake's western shore. Unlike many lakeside towns, Tignale sits at a higher altitude, offering sweeping views and a cooler climate. It is an excellent destination for hiking, as numerous trails lead through forests, olive groves, and mountain pastures.

One of the main attractions in Tignale is the Sanctuary of Montecastello, a hilltop monastery with a history dating back to the 13th century. The sanctuary is known for its beautiful frescoes and peaceful setting, as well as the panoramic view from its terrace. The climb to the sanctuary is steep but rewarding, and it remains a place of pilgrimage for locals.

Tignale is also well known for its olive oil production. The combination of mountain air and Mediterranean sunshine creates ideal conditions for high-quality olive oil. Visitors can tour local olive mills and sample some of the best oil in the region.

## Gargnano's Historic Center

Gargnano is a small town on the western shore of Lake Garda that has retained much of its original character. Unlike many other villages, it has avoided large-scale tourism development, allowing it to maintain a peaceful and authentic feel.

The town is known for its grand villas, many of which were built in the 18th and 19th centuries by wealthy families from Brescia and Verona. Villa Bettoni, one of the most impressive estates, has beautifully landscaped gardens and a striking Baroque facade.

Gargnano is also historically significant for its role during World War II, when it served as a base for Benito Mussolini's government-in-exile. Some buildings from that period still stand, adding an unexpected historical element to the town.

The village's waterfront is lined with small fishing boats, and it remains one of the best places on the lake to experience the traditional way of life. Restaurants here focus on simple, high-quality ingredients, often featuring fish from the lake, local cheeses, and citrus fruits grown in nearby orchards.

For those looking for a quiet and authentic experience, Gargnano offers a balance of history, scenic beauty, and local culture without the crowds found in other parts of Lake Garda.

Each of these villages has its own unique character, shaped by centuries of history and the natural beauty of the lake. They provide an alternative to the busier towns, offering a chance to experience the true essence of Lake Garda in a more personal and relaxed way.

## 8.1.2 Best Secluded Scenic Spots

Lake Garda is filled with breathtaking scenery, but many of its most popular viewpoints and natural sites attract crowds, especially during peak travel seasons. For those looking for a more peaceful experience, there are still many hidden spots where you can enjoy the beauty of the lake away from the hustle and bustle. These secluded locations range from quiet beaches and panoramic viewpoints to hidden valleys and forest trails, offering a chance to take in the landscape without distraction.

### Punta Larici

Punta Larici is one of the most dramatic viewpoints on Lake Garda, yet it remains relatively undiscovered compared to other scenic spots. It is located on the western shore near Pregasina, a small hamlet above Riva del Garda. The viewpoint offers a sweeping view of the lake stretching all the way to the southern shores, with sheer cliffs dropping into the water below.

Reaching Punta Larici requires a moderate hike from Pregasina, taking about an hour along a well-marked trail. The route winds through pine forests and opens up to rocky cliffs, rewarding hikers with stunning sights at the top. Since it is not as well known as other viewpoints, you are likely to find yourself alone or with only a few other visitors, making it an ideal spot for those seeking tranquility.

### Baia delle Sirene (Mermaid's Bay)

Baia delle Sirene is a hidden cove on the eastern shore of the lake, just north of Garda town. Unlike the busier beaches in the area, this bay offers a quiet setting surrounded by olive groves and shaded areas.

The crystal-clear water and smooth pebble beach make it one of the best places for swimming in a peaceful environment.

While Baia delle Sirene is privately managed, there is an entrance fee that helps limit the number of visitors, keeping the atmosphere calm. Sun loungers and umbrellas are available for rent, but many people prefer to bring their own towels and find a shaded spot under the olive trees. Arriving early in the morning or later in the afternoon ensures an even more secluded experience.

**Valle delle Cartiere**
For those interested in a mix of history and nature, Valle delle Cartiere (Valley of the Paper Mills) near Toscolano Maderno is a perfect choice. This quiet valley was once home to a thriving paper industry, and the ruins of old mills are still visible along the trail. The valley is now a peaceful retreat with walking paths that follow a stream, passing by waterfalls and abandoned stone structures.

The trail is relatively easy and can be completed in a couple of hours, making it a great option for those looking for a relaxed walk through nature. The sound of flowing water, combined with the shade from surrounding forests, makes Valle delle Cartiere an excellent escape from the heat during summer.

**Monte Bestone**
Monte Bestone is a lesser-known viewpoint located above Limone sul Garda. It offers panoramic views of the northern part of the lake, framed by the dramatic peaks of the surrounding mountains. Unlike the more famous Monte Baldo, which attracts many visitors, Monte Bestone remains quiet, even during high season.

Hiking to the summit takes about 90 minutes from the starting point near Vesio. The path is relatively steep in some areas but is manageable for those with moderate hiking experience. At the top, there is a wooden bench where you can sit and take in the view in complete solitude. On clear days, you can see all the way to Sirmione on the southern shore.

## Corno di Reamol

Corno di Reamol is a hidden cliffside spot located just north of Limone sul Garda. It is accessible via a small path that branches off from the lakeside road. This secluded area offers a unique perspective of the lake, with towering rock formations creating a dramatic contrast against the deep blue water.

This location is best suited for those who enjoy off-the-beaten-path adventures. There are no designated trails or signs leading to Corno di Reamol, making it feel like a true hidden gem. The spot is particularly stunning at sunset when the cliffs cast long shadows over the lake, creating a peaceful and almost surreal atmosphere.

## Sentiero Busatte-Tempesta

For those looking for a scenic walk away from the crowds, the Sentiero Busatte-Tempesta trail on the eastern shore of the lake is an excellent choice. This route runs along the cliffs above the water, offering stunning views without the large tourist presence found in other hiking areas. The trail includes sections of metal staircases attached to the rock face, giving it an adventurous feel while still being safe for most hikers.

The path starts near Torbole and takes about two hours to complete. Since it is a linear route, many hikers choose to turn back at a certain point rather than walking the entire way. The lack of road access along the trail means it remains quiet and free from motorized noise, allowing visitors to fully enjoy the natural beauty of the lake.

Each of these secluded scenic spots offers a different way to experience Lake Garda, whether it's through hiking, swimming, or simply sitting in silence and taking in the view. These places allow for a deeper connection with the landscape, away from the crowds that often gather in the more well-known locations.

# Culture, Arts, and Music

## Local Festivals and Celebrations

Lake Garda's cultural richness is evident in its many festivals, where history, tradition, and local identity come alive through music, food, and celebrations. Throughout the year, towns along the lake host events that reflect centuries-old customs, religious devotion, and the region's deep appreciation for the arts and cuisine. Many of these gatherings are tied to the lake's agricultural heritage, honoring wine, olives, lemons, and fish, while others commemorate historical moments and local saints. These festivals provide a deeper understanding of life around Lake Garda, offering visitors a chance to witness authentic traditions in stunning settings.

**Wine and Food Festivals**
The fertile lands surrounding Lake Garda produce some of Italy's finest wines and olive oils, and several festivals celebrate these prized local products.
**1. Festa dell'Uva e del Vino (Grape and Wine Festival) – Bardolino:** Every autumn, Bardolino comes alive with its famous Grape and Wine Festival, held along the waterfront promenade. This event, typically in late September or early October, is a tribute to the region's rich winemaking heritage. Visitors can sample Bardolino wines, known for their light and fruity notes, while enjoying regional dishes such as risotto with Amarone and fresh-caught fish from the lake. Music, folk dancing, and boat parades add to the festive atmosphere, culminating in a spectacular fireworks display over the water.
**2. Festa dell'Olio (Olive Oil Festival) – Torri del Benaco:** In November, Torri del Benaco honors its tradition of olive oil production with the Festa dell'Olio. This festival showcases extra virgin olive oil from the surrounding hills, known for its delicate flavor and high quality. Local producers set up stalls where visitors can taste freshly pressed oil, often paired with homemade bread and regional cheeses. Cooking demonstrations, guided tastings, and

• • •

educational workshops provide insight into the importance of olive oil in Lake Garda's cuisine.

**3. Festa del Pesce (Fish Festival) – Garda:** Garda's Fish Festival, held in early August, highlights the town's connection to the lake's fishing heritage. Freshly grilled trout, whitefish, and sardines are served in outdoor dining areas, accompanied by local wines. The festival also features demonstrations of traditional fishing techniques, live music performances, and an exhibition on the history of fishing in the region.

**Historical and Religious Festivals**

Many festivals around Lake Garda have deep religious significance, honoring patron saints with grand processions, ceremonies, and community gatherings.

**1. Sagra di San Benedetto – Limone sul Garda:** In July, Limone sul Garda pays tribute to its patron saint, San Benedetto, with a multi-day festival. The event includes religious processions through the town's historic streets, traditional music performances, and food stalls offering local specialties. The highlight is a torch-lit boat procession along the lake, followed by a fireworks display. This festival is a great opportunity to experience Limone's close-knit community and its devotion to its heritage.

**2. Festa di Santa Maria Maddalena – Torri del Benaco:** Torri del Benaco celebrates its patron saint, Santa Maria Maddalena, every July with a lively waterfront festival. A key feature is the lake procession, where a statue of the saint is carried through the harbor on a decorated boat, accompanied by a fleet of smaller boats. The town's streets fill with musicians, dancers, and food vendors, while local restaurants serve special dishes prepared just for the occasion.

**3. Sant'Ercolano Festival – Toscolano Maderno:** In August, Toscolano Maderno honors Sant'Ercolano, the protector of fishermen, with a festival that blends faith and celebration. The event includes a solemn Mass, a boat procession on the lake, and a feast featuring freshly caught fish. The festival ends with a grand fireworks show, reflecting on the water.

## Cultural and Artistic Festivals
Lake Garda's love for art, literature, and music is evident in its cultural festivals, which feature performances, exhibitions, and creative workshops.

**1. Notte di Fiaba (Fairy Tale Night) – Riva del Garda:** Held in late August, Notte di Fiaba transforms Riva del Garda into a magical world inspired by classic fairy tales. Each year, the festival follows a different literary theme, with costumed performers, storytelling sessions, and interactive theater productions. Families can enjoy street performances, puppet shows, and workshops for children. The festival culminates in an impressive fireworks show over the lake.

**2. Garda Music Festival – Various Locations:** The Garda Music Festival takes place in several towns around the lake throughout the summer, featuring concerts in historic churches, open-air amphitheaters, and villa gardens. The program includes classical, jazz, folk, and contemporary music, drawing both renowned musicians and emerging artists. Sirmione, Bardolino, and Salò are among the key locations that host performances.

**3. Fiera di San Michele – Moniga del Garda:** The San Michele Fair, held in Moniga del Garda in September, is a tribute to traditional rural life. It features agricultural exhibitions, livestock displays, and food tastings that celebrate the region's farming heritage. Folk music and dance performances add to the lively atmosphere, making it a great way to experience local traditions.

## Sporting and Adventure Festivals
Lake Garda's natural beauty makes it a hub for outdoor sports, and several events highlight activities such as sailing, rowing, and endurance races.

**1. Palio delle Bisse – Historical Rowing Race:** One of the most exciting events on Lake Garda is the Palio delle Bisse, a traditional Venetian-style rowing race held in various towns from June to August. The race features teams rowing in "bisse," long wooden boats reminiscent of those used in the 16th century. Each town fields its own team, creating a competitive yet festive atmosphere. The grand finale, usually held in Peschiera del Garda, attracts large crowds cheering for their local rowers.

**2. Lake Garda Marathon – Malcesine to Limone sul Garda:** For running enthusiasts, the Lake Garda Marathon in October is a stunning event. The course stretches from Malcesine to Limone sul Garda, offering breathtaking views of the lake along the way. Runners pass through tunnels, lakeside paths, and small villages, making this one of the most scenic marathons in Italy.

**3. Windsurfing and Sailing Festivals – Torbole and Riva del Garda:** The northern shores of Lake Garda, particularly in Torbole and Riva del Garda, are famous for their strong winds, making them a prime location for windsurfing and sailing events. Competitions such as the Riva Cup and Torbole Wind Festival attract athletes from around the world, showcasing the skill and excitement of these water sports. Visitors can watch races from the shore or take lessons from local schools to try the sport themselves.

Lake Garda's festivals offer a true taste of the region's character, blending centuries-old traditions with modern celebrations. From wine tastings and historic regattas to artistic performances and religious feasts, these events bring the towns to life in a way that makes every visit more memorable.

## Artistic Expressions of Lake Garda

Lake Garda's natural beauty has long inspired artists, writers, and performers, making it a hub for creativity. The towns around the lake celebrate artistic traditions through galleries, public art, festivals, and performances. From classical paintings to contemporary sculptures, from literary works to live theater, the artistic expressions of Lake Garda reflect its deep cultural roots and the ever-evolving creative spirit of its people.

**Historical Influence on Art**
Artists have been drawn to Lake Garda for centuries, captivated by its shimmering waters, dramatic mountains, and picturesque towns. During the Renaissance, painters and sculptors created works influenced by the religious and architectural beauty of the region. The Venetian influence is particularly strong, especially in towns like Sirmione and Peschiera del Garda, where elements of Venetian art and design can still be seen in historic buildings and churches.

Several famous painters have depicted Lake Garda in their works. In the 19th and early 20th centuries, landscape artists from Germany and Austria visited the lake, drawn by its Mediterranean climate and changing light. Their paintings captured the tranquility of the water, the olive groves, and the colorful facades of lakeside villages.

**Art Galleries and Museums**
Lake Garda's appreciation for visual arts is evident in its many galleries and museums.
**1. Museo di Salò (MUSA) – Salò:** The MUSA in Salò houses an impressive collection of art, history, and culture from the region. Exhibitions include works by Italian painters, historical artifacts, and contemporary installations. The museum also hosts temporary exhibits featuring local and international artists.
**2. Galleria Civica G. B. Bosio – Desenzano del Garda:** This gallery in Desenzano del Garda showcases modern and contemporary art, with a focus on Italian artists. The rotating exhibitions feature paintings, photography, and sculptures, highlighting different artistic movements.
**3. Casa del Podestà – Lonato del Garda:** This historic residence in Lonato del Garda is home to a vast collection of paintings, sculptures, and manuscripts. The building itself, with its frescoed ceilings and Renaissance architecture, is a work of art. The collection includes religious art, portraits, and decorative pieces from the 16th to the 19th centuries.

**Street Art and Public Installations**
While Lake Garda is known for its classical art, contemporary creativity can be found in the form of murals, sculptures, and street performances.
**1. The Open-Air Art of Malcesine:** Malcesine, with its medieval charm, features a growing number of outdoor art installations. Local artists have contributed to the town's aesthetic by painting murals on building facades, depicting historical scenes and modern interpretations of lake life.
**2. Artistic Walk in Riva del Garda:** Riva del Garda has introduced public sculptures along its waterfront, blending modern art with nature.

These pieces, often abstract, reflect the movement of water and wind, adding a contemporary touch to the historic town.

**3. Tignale's Artistic Benches:** The small town of Tignale has transformed everyday objects into art. Local artists have painted benches throughout the town, each one telling a different story. These benches feature landscapes, portraits, and abstract designs, creating an open-air gallery that blends with the town's peaceful atmosphere.

**Literary Connections to Lake Garda**

Lake Garda has also inspired writers and poets throughout history. The Roman poet Catullus, who lived in Sirmione, wrote about the lake's beauty. His villa ruins still stand today, offering insight into the literary history of the region.

In more recent history, the German writer Johann Wolfgang von Goethe visited Lake Garda in the late 18th century and described its landscapes in his travel writings. D. H. Lawrence, the English novelist, spent time in Gargnano and wrote about the lake's atmosphere and the daily life of its people.

Today, literary events and book festivals continue to honor Lake Garda's connection to storytelling. Writers' retreats and poetry readings are held in scenic locations, offering inspiration to modern authors.

**Live Performances and Music**

Lake Garda's artistic expression is not limited to visual art—it thrives in music, theater, and dance.

**1. Arena di Verona Performances:** While not directly on the lake, the Arena di Verona is a short distance away and hosts world-famous opera performances. Many visitors to Lake Garda take an evening trip to Verona to experience opera in the ancient Roman amphitheater.

**2. Sirmione in Musica:** Sirmione hosts an annual music festival featuring classical concerts in historical settings, including the Scaliger Castle and local churches. The performances range from orchestral pieces to solo recitals, blending music with the architectural elegance of the town.

**3. Theater and Street Performances in Lazise:** Lazise's town square often transforms into a stage for open-air theater and street performances. Local actors and musicians bring historical stories to life, reenacting legends and folklore from the region.

Lake Garda's artistic scene is a blend of history and modern creativity. From museum exhibitions to street art, from literary inspiration to live performances, the lake continues to be a source of artistic expression that evolves while honoring its rich cultural heritage.

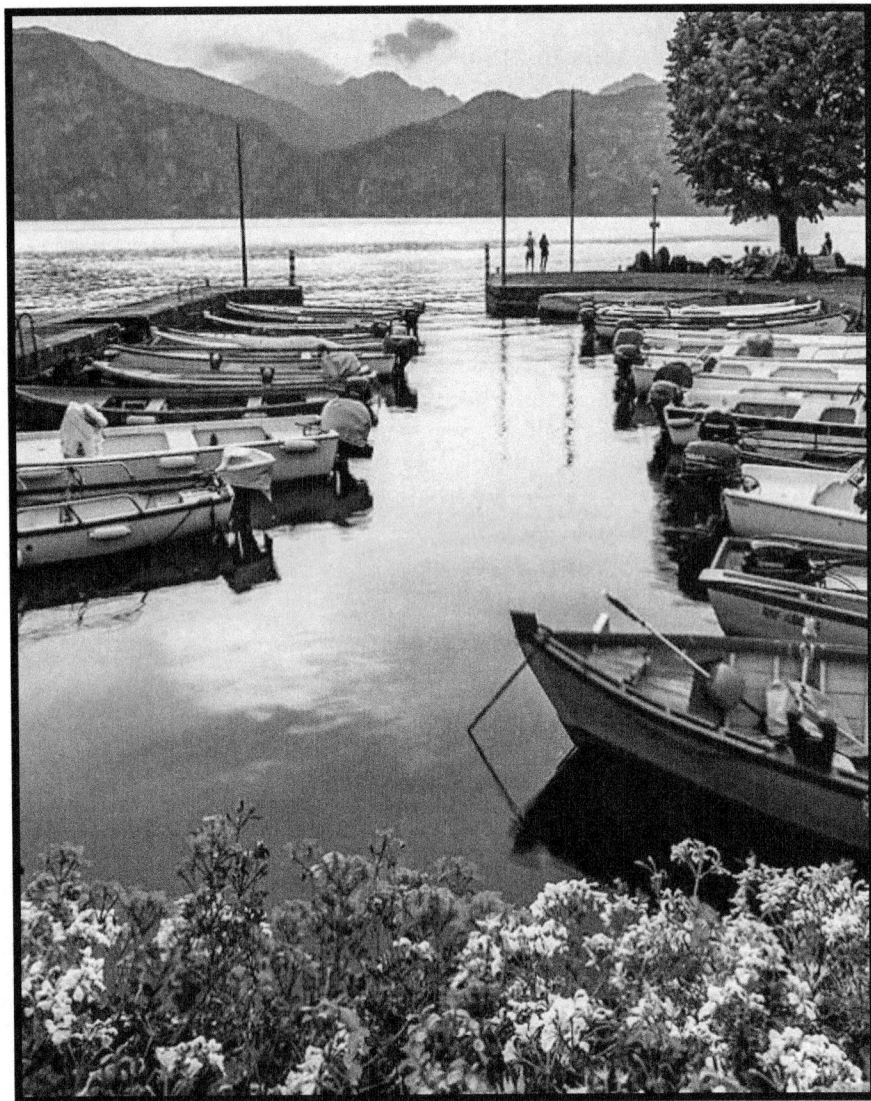

# CHAPTER 9: OUTDOOR ADVENTURES & ACTIVITIES

## Trekking and Hiking Routes

## Most Popular Hiking Trails

Lake Garda offers a mix of scenic trails that cater to all levels of hikers. From challenging mountain routes to scenic lakeside paths, these trails provide stunning views, fresh air, and a closer connection to the natural surroundings. The most popular routes often include a mix of history, dramatic landscapes, and well-marked paths that ensure a smooth experience.

### Monte Baldo Ridge Trail
Monte Baldo is one of the most famous hiking destinations in the region. The ridge offers panoramic views of the lake, stretching across the horizon with the Alps in the background.
- **Starting Point:** Funivia Malcesine-Monte Baldo Cable Car Station
- **Distance:** Varies (multiple routes from 5 km to 20 km)
- **Difficulty:** Moderate to challenging

➡ **Highlights:** Alpine meadows, wildflowers, and views extending into the Dolomites.

Many hikers take the cable car from Malcesine to the upper station and then walk along the ridge. Some opt for longer trails leading down to the villages below, offering a mix of mountain and forest scenery.

### Sentiero Busatte-Tempesta

This trail is known for its dramatic metal staircases built into the cliffs, offering uninterrupted views over Lake Garda.

➡ **Starting Point:** Busatte Park, Torbole
➡ **Distance:** 4 km one way
➡ **Difficulty:** Moderate
➡ **Highlights:** Panoramic lake views, iron staircases, and limestone cliffs.

The route follows the eastern shore's rugged terrain, providing a dynamic landscape of forests and rocky outcrops. It's an excellent choice for hikers looking for a shorter but rewarding experience.

### Strada della Forra

Considered one of the most scenic routes in Italy, this trail follows the dramatic gorge that Winston Churchill once called "the eighth wonder of the world."

➡ **Starting Point:** Pieve di Tremosine
➡ **Distance:** Approximately 6 km
➡ **Difficulty:** Moderate
➡ **Highlights:** Narrow canyons, waterfalls, and ancient stone bridges.

This trail winds through a deep gorge, with rock walls rising on both sides. It's a mix of paved pathways and rugged terrain, making it a unique blend of natural beauty and historical significance.

### Cima Comer and the Bocca di Nevese

This route provides a mix of dense forest, open meadows, and stunning lake views from the summit.

➡ **Starting Point:** Gargnano
➡ **Distance:** 10 km round trip
➡ **Difficulty:** Moderate to challenging

⇨ **Highlights:** 360-degree views, wildlife, and diverse landscapes. Hikers pass through chestnut forests before reaching open pastures that lead to the summit. The final stretch provides sweeping views of the lake and surrounding valleys.

### Sentiero della Ponale

One of the most famous scenic walks around Lake Garda, this route follows an old road carved into the cliffs above the water.

⇨ **Starting Point:** Riva del Garda
⇨ **Distance:** 10 km round trip
⇨ **Difficulty:** Easy to moderate
⇨ **Highlights:** Lakefront tunnels, historic fortifications, and breathtaking drop-offs.

This trail is popular with both hikers and cyclists. It's an excellent option for those looking for a scenic route without a steep incline.

### Rocca di Manerba Trail

This shorter hike leads to a famous viewpoint overlooking the lake and surrounding countryside.

⇨ **Starting Point:** Manerba del Garda
⇨ **Distance:** 3 km loop
⇨ **Difficulty:** Easy
⇨ **Highlights:** Archaeological remains, a panoramic viewpoint, and a protected nature reserve.

The trail winds through Mediterranean vegetation before reaching a rocky plateau with one of the most scenic lake views in the region. It's a great option for families and those looking for a relaxed but rewarding walk.

## Lesser-Known Nature Walks

For those looking to escape the more crowded paths, Lake Garda offers several lesser-known trails that provide solitude and stunning natural beauty. These routes often take hikers through peaceful forests, hidden valleys, and quiet hilltops, offering a more secluded experience.

### Eremo di San Valentino Trail

A peaceful route leading to a hidden hermitage built into the cliffs, this trail is perfect for those seeking solitude and history.

⇨ **Starting Point:** Gargnano
⇨ **Distance:** 6 km round trip
⇨ **Difficulty:** Moderate
⇨ **Highlights:** A historic hermitage, panoramic lake views, and a quiet forest setting.

The hermitage, built in the 1600s, provides a unique cultural touch to the hike. The surrounding forest keeps much of the trail shaded, making it a great option even in warmer months.

### Valle delle Cartiere

A journey through an ancient paper mill valley, this hike combines nature and history in an off-the-beaten-path setting.

⇨ **Starting Point:** Toscolano-Maderno
⇨ **Distance:** 5 km loop
⇨ **Difficulty:** Easy to moderate
⇨ **Highlights:** Ruins of old paper mills, a flowing river, and a peaceful gorge.

The route follows the Toscolano River, leading through abandoned industrial sites where paper was once produced. Signs along the path explain the area's history, making it an informative and scenic walk.

### Monte Bestone Trail

A lesser-known viewpoint that offers a breathtaking view of Lake Garda without the crowds.

⇨ **Starting Point:** Limone sul Garda
⇨ **Distance:** 8 km round trip
⇨ **Difficulty:** Moderate
⇨ **Highlights:** Wildflower meadows, panoramic viewpoints, and a peaceful forest.

The trail winds through quiet meadows and eventually leads to a viewpoint with a stunning angle over the northern part of the lake. It's a great alternative for those looking to avoid the busier Monte Baldo trails.

## Corna Vecchia and Cima Rest

This route takes hikers through mountain pastures and traditional alpine huts, offering an authentic experience of the region's rural life.

➪ **Starting Point:** Magasa
➪ **Distance:** 12 km round trip
➪ **Difficulty:** Moderate to challenging
➪ **Highlights:** Traditional mountain huts, alpine meadows, and views of the Brenta Dolomites.

It's a rewarding hike with a mix of history and natural beauty. The pastures along the route are still used for grazing, and some huts sell local cheese and honey during the summer months.

## Madonna della Corona Pilgrimage Trail

This spiritual walk leads to one of the most unique religious sites in Italy, a sanctuary built into the cliffs.

➪ **Starting Point:** Brentino Belluno
➪ **Distance:** 8 km round trip
➪ **Difficulty:** Moderate
➪ **Highlights:** A dramatic cliffside church, a serene atmosphere, and a well-maintained path.

Pilgrims and hikers alike follow this route, drawn by its peaceful surroundings and cultural significance. The sanctuary, perched against the rock face, is a remarkable sight after the uphill journey.

## Monte Pizzocolo Trail

A remote peak with some of the best panoramic views in the region, this hike is a rewarding challenge for those looking for solitude.

➪ **Starting Point:** San Michele
➪ **Distance:** 14 km round trip
➪ **Difficulty:** Challenging
➪ **Highlights:** Views stretching to the Apennines, untouched forests, and occasional wildlife sightings.

The summit provides one of the most impressive perspectives of Lake Garda. Due to its difficulty and length, it's less frequented, making it ideal for experienced hikers looking for a quieter trail.

These lesser-known routes offer a refreshing alternative to the more crowded paths, giving hikers the opportunity to experience Lake Garda's landscapes in a more tranquil setting.

# Lake Sports and Water Adventures

## Paddleboarding and Kayaking

Lake Garda's calm mornings and scenic shoreline make it an excellent destination for paddleboarding and kayaking. The lake's size means that there are a variety of routes, from gentle paddles along sheltered coves to more adventurous journeys across open waters.

### Best Spots for Paddleboarding and Kayaking
- ➪ **Riva del Garda** – The northern part of the lake is ideal for those looking for adventure. With towering cliffs and deep waters, it's a dramatic setting for paddling. The early mornings are the best time for calm conditions before the wind picks up.
- ➪ **Sirmione** – Paddling around the peninsula offers a unique experience, passing beneath the historic Scaliger Castle and near the Grotte di Catullo, ancient Roman ruins. The shallow waters in some areas make it accessible for beginners.
- ➪ **Gargnano** – A quieter section of the lake with a rugged shoreline and small beaches, perfect for a more relaxed paddle.
- ➪ **Isola del Garda** – Paddling around this private island provides views of its stunning villa and gardens. Some guided tours allow for stops near the island.
- ➪ **Baia delle Sirene** – This scenic bay near Garda is one of the most beautiful areas to paddle, offering clear water and a peaceful atmosphere.

### Paddleboarding on Lake Garda
Paddleboarding has become increasingly popular due to its accessibility and the unique perspective it offers on the lake's landscape. Beginners can take lessons from rental shops in towns like Bardolino, Lazise, and Malcesine. More experienced paddleboarders may enjoy an early morning session when the lake is at its calmest, or

a sunset paddle for a stunning view of the changing colors over the water.

For those looking for an extra challenge, SUP yoga sessions are available in some locations, combining balance and relaxation with the lake's gentle movement.

## Kayaking Adventures

Kayaking on Lake Garda offers a more stable and faster way to cover longer distances, making it a great way to reach hidden coves and less crowded areas. There are both single and tandem kayaks available for rent, and some guided tours focus on historical sites or natural landmarks.

⇨ **Short Routes for Beginners** – Paddling along the shores of Bardolino or Lazise is a good introduction to kayaking on the lake. The waters here tend to be calm, and there are plenty of places to take a break along the way.

⇨ **Intermediate Routes** – More experienced kayakers might enjoy the stretch between Malcesine and Cassone, passing by small harbors and scenic viewpoints. Another great option is heading from Limone sul Garda towards the towering cliffs of the northern section.

⇨ **Longer Routes** – Adventurous kayakers can attempt to cross sections of the lake or paddle from one town to another. The stretch between Torri del Benaco and Sirmione is a rewarding challenge with changing landscapes along the way.

## Rentals and Guided Tours

Rental shops are widely available in towns like Riva del Garda, Sirmione, Bardolino, and Malcesine. Many offer hourly or full-day rentals, as well as guided excursions for those looking for a structured experience. Some tours include stops at caves, historical sites, or even local restaurants for a lakeside meal.

Kayaking and paddleboarding are among the best ways to enjoy Lake Garda's tranquil side. With plenty of options for all skill levels, these activities allow visitors to experience the water in a peaceful and active way.

## Sailing and Wind Sports

Lake Garda's reliable winds and open waters have made it one of Europe's top destinations for sailing, windsurfing, and kitesurfing. The unique wind patterns create excellent conditions for both beginners and experienced athletes, with different parts of the lake catering to varying skill levels.

### Understanding Lake Garda's Winds

- **Pelèr** – A strong morning wind that blows from the north, usually starting at sunrise and lasting until midday. It creates ideal conditions for sailing and advanced wind sports.
- **Ora** – A more moderate afternoon wind from the south, typically beginning after lunch and continuing until evening. This is the perfect wind for beginner windsurfers and sailors.

### Sailing on Lake Garda

Sailing is one of the most traditional water activities on the lake, and many towns have marinas with rental services and sailing schools.

### Best Towns for Sailing

- **Riva del Garda** – A major hub for sailing, with multiple regattas and events throughout the year. The combination of the Pelèr and Ora winds provides consistent conditions.
- **Torri del Benaco** – A scenic starting point for sailing excursions, with a picturesque harbor and views of the eastern shoreline.
- **Gargnano** – Home to the famous Centomiglia Regatta, this town has a strong sailing culture and offers lessons and boat rentals.
- **Desenzano del Garda** – A good location for relaxed sailing, with marinas offering rentals for those looking to explore at their own pace.

Both private charters and group sailing excursions are available for those who want to experience the lake under sail without handling the boat themselves. Many tours offer sunset sailing or half-day trips with stops for swimming and dining.

### Windsurfing and Kitesurfing

The northern part of Lake Garda, particularly around Riva del Garda and Torbole, is famous for windsurfing and kitesurfing. The combination of reliable winds and a strong watersports culture has made this area a prime destination for enthusiasts from across Europe.

**Best Spots for Windsurfing**

⇨ **Torbole** – One of the most famous windsurfing locations in Italy, with rental shops and schools lining the waterfront. The steady Ora wind in the afternoon is perfect for learners.

⇨ **Malcesine** – Offers a mix of conditions for different levels, with both morning and afternoon winds creating opportunities for skill progression.

⇨ **Riva del Garda** – A great place for more experienced windsurfers, with stronger winds and an active windsurfing community.

Windsurfing schools in these towns provide lessons for beginners, as well as rental equipment for those with experience. Many schools offer multi-day courses to help visitors improve their technique.

**Kitesurfing Hotspots**

⇨ **Campione del Garda** – One of the best places for kitesurfing, with dedicated launch areas and professional schools.

⇨ **Navene (near Malcesine)** – A quieter location with good wind conditions for kitesurfers looking for more space.

Since kitesurfing requires specific conditions and safety considerations, it's recommended to take lessons or join guided sessions before attempting it solo. Many operators use boat-assisted launching to help kitesurfers get out onto the lake more efficiently.

**Regattas and Events**

Lake Garda hosts some of the most important sailing events in Italy, attracting sailors from around the world.

⇨ **Centomiglia Regatta** – A prestigious long-distance sailing race held annually in Gargnano, drawing professional and amateur sailors alike.

⇨ **Lake Garda Meeting Optimist Class** – One of the largest youth sailing competitions, held in Riva del Garda.

⇨ **Foiling Week** – A high-tech sailing event featuring hydrofoil boats, held in Malcesine.

For those interested in competitive sailing or just wanting to watch professional sailors in action, these events provide a great opportunity to experience the lake's sporting culture.

Sailing, windsurfing, and kitesurfing are some of the most exhilarating ways to experience Lake Garda. With its unique wind patterns and world-class facilities, the lake offers ideal conditions for both relaxed sailing excursions and high-energy wind sports.

# Cycling and Mountain Biking

## Best Biking Trails Around the Lake

Cycling around Lake Garda offers an incredible mix of easy lakeside rides, scenic countryside routes, and challenging mountain trails. The variety of terrain makes it a fantastic destination for cyclists of all skill levels. Whether you're looking for a relaxed ride along the shoreline or an adrenaline-fueled mountain biking experience, there's a trail suited for you.

**Lakeside Cycling Paths**
For those who prefer a smooth ride with breathtaking water views, Lake Garda's lakeside paths are an excellent choice. These routes are mostly paved, making them suitable for families, casual cyclists, and anyone who wants to enjoy a leisurely ride.

➪ **Garda to Bardolino to Lazise** – One of the most popular cycling routes along the eastern shore, this path runs parallel to the lake, offering stunning waterfront scenery. The route is mostly flat and well-maintained, making it ideal for beginners. Along the way, you'll pass olive groves, vineyards, and charming lakeside villages where you can stop for a coffee or a gelato.

➪ **Sirmione Peninsula Ride** – A shorter but scenic ride that allows cyclists to explore the famous Sirmione peninsula. Starting from Desenzano or Peschiera del Garda, this route takes you along quiet roads with views of the Scaliger Castle and the surrounding blue waters. It's a great choice for a relaxing morning ride.

➪ **Limone sul Garda to Riva del Garda** – A section of the new **Garda by Bike** project, this trail features the breathtaking

**Cycling Path of Dreams**, a suspended cycling path built along the cliffs of Limone. The ride offers unparalleled lake views and is one of the most scenic stretches for cyclists looking for a relaxed but visually stunning experience.

## Countryside and Vineyard Routes

For those looking to combine cycling with the charm of rural landscapes, the inland trails leading through vineyards, rolling hills, and medieval villages are perfect. These routes often include gentle climbs and a few dirt paths, making them enjoyable for intermediate riders.

➡ **Valtenesi Wine Route** – This loop in the western part of the lake takes cyclists through the Valtenesi region, known for its olive groves, historic castles, and renowned wineries. The route passes through charming villages like Polpenazze del Garda and San Felice del Benaco, with opportunities to stop for a wine tasting or a traditional meal.

➡ **Mori to Torbole** – Following the old railway route from Mori to the northern shores of Lake Garda, this path leads cyclists through vineyards and picturesque countryside before descending into Torbole. The gentle slopes and paved roads make it a comfortable ride for those looking for a scenic countryside experience.

## Mountain Biking Trails

For experienced riders looking for a challenge, the mountains surrounding Lake Garda provide some of the best mountain biking trails in Italy. These routes feature steep climbs, rocky descents, and rewarding panoramic views.

➡ **Sentiero della Ponale** – One of the most famous mountain biking routes in the region, the Ponale Trail connects Riva del Garda to Ledro Valley. The trail follows a historic military road carved into the cliffs, offering sweeping views of the lake below. The ascent is steady but manageable, making it a favorite among both mountain bikers and gravel riders.

➡ **Monte Baldo Trails** – The slopes of Monte Baldo offer a variety of challenging routes, including technical single tracks and downhill descents. Many riders take the **Malcesine cable car** up the mountain and then ride down, experiencing different terrain types on the way. These trails are recommended for skilled mountain bikers due to the steep gradients and rocky sections.

➡ **Tremalzo Pass** – A legendary trail for mountain bikers, Tremalzo is known for its high-altitude gravel paths and breathtaking views. The ride starts from Lake Ledro and climbs up through alpine landscapes, eventually reaching one of the best viewpoints over Lake Garda. The descent is fast and thrilling, making it a rewarding experience for adventurous cyclists.

## Bike Rentals and Guided Tours

Cycling around Lake Garda is made easy by the numerous bike rental shops and guided tours available throughout the region. Whether you need a high-performance road bike, a sturdy mountain bike, or an electric bike for a more relaxed ride, there are plenty of options to choose from.

**Where to Rent a Bike**

Many towns around the lake have reputable bike rental shops that offer a variety of bicycles and equipment. Most shops provide helmets, repair kits, and detailed maps of recommended routes.

➡ **Riva del Garda** – One of the best spots to rent a bike, with multiple shops catering to road cyclists and mountain bikers. Stores like Garda Bike Shop and Moser Sport offer high-quality bikes for rent, including full-suspension mountain bikes and carbon road bikes.

➡ **Torri del Benaco** – A quieter town with several rental options, great for those planning to explore the eastern shore or take on Monte Baldo trails.

➡ **Sirmione and Desenzano** – Ideal locations for renting city bikes or e-bikes for relaxed rides along the southern shore. Shops like Bike Rent Desenzano and Garda South Cycling provide a good range of options.

➡ **Malcesine** – Perfect for those wanting to take the cable car up Monte Baldo and ride down. Bike rental shops here often have specialized mountain biking equipment, including protective gear.

**Electric Bikes (E-Bikes) and Accessibility**
For those who want to enjoy cycling without worrying about steep climbs, e-bikes are a fantastic option. Many rental shops now offer electric bikes, allowing cyclists of all fitness levels to tackle longer routes and higher elevations with ease. Towns like Bardolino, Lazise, and Peschiera del Garda have e-bike rental stations, making it simple to explore the lake without too much effort.

**Guided Cycling Tours**
For travelers who prefer a structured experience, guided cycling tours are an excellent way to discover Lake Garda's best routes with local experts. These tours often include bike rentals, support vehicles, and knowledgeable guides who share insights about the region's history, culture, and natural beauty.

➪ **Wine and Gastronomy Bike Tours** – Many companies offer guided tours that combine cycling with stops at local wineries and farmhouses. These tours typically cover routes in the Valtenesi and Bardolino wine regions, offering a mix of scenic cycling and delicious food tastings.

➪ **Monte Baldo Mountain Biking Excursions** – Local guides lead mountain bikers through the best trails on Monte Baldo, ensuring a safe and exhilarating ride. These tours often start with a cable car ride up the mountain and include technical training for those new to downhill biking.

➪ **Sunset Lakeside Rides** – Some companies offer evening rides along the lake, allowing cyclists to experience the beautiful changing colors over the water while riding along quiet paths. These tours are usually designed for all skill levels and often include a stop at a lakeside café.

**Multi-Day Cycling Trips**
For serious cyclists looking to explore the region in depth, multi-day cycling trips around Lake Garda and beyond are available. These longer tours often include accommodation, luggage transport, and a mix of road and off-road cycling experiences.

➡️ **Garda to Verona Cycling Trip** – A popular option for those wanting to combine Lake Garda's landscapes with a visit to the historic city of Verona. This route follows gentle countryside roads and offers plenty of cultural and gastronomic stops along the way.

➡️ **Dolomites to Lake Garda Adventure** – A more challenging trip that starts in the Dolomites and descends towards Lake Garda, covering high-altitude passes and scenic valleys before reaching the lake's shores.

With its mix of well-paved cycling paths, scenic countryside routes, and world-class mountain biking trails, Lake Garda is a paradise for cyclists. Rentals and guided tours make it easy for visitors to experience the lake on two wheels.

# Relaxation and Wellness

## The Best Spa Retreats in Lake Garda

Lake Garda is home to some of Italy's finest spa retreats, offering a perfect blend of natural beauty and relaxation. The region's thermal springs, mineral-rich waters, and high-end wellness centers attract visitors looking to unwind in serene surroundings. Whether you prefer luxurious thermal spas, lakeside resorts, or holistic wellness centers, Lake Garda has something to offer.

**Thermal Spas and Natural Hot Springs**
One of the unique features of Lake Garda's wellness scene is its thermal waters, known for their healing properties. These waters, rich in minerals, have been used for centuries to promote relaxation and well-being.

➡️ **Terme di Sirmione** – One of the most famous thermal spas in Italy, Terme di Sirmione is located on the southern shore of the lake. The spa's water comes from the Boiola spring, known for its sulfur and bromine content, which is believed to help with respiratory and skin conditions. Visitors can enjoy a variety of thermal pools, hydromassage circuits, and steam baths, all set against the backdrop of Sirmione's medieval charm.

● ● ●

⇨ **Garda Thermal Park (Parco Termale del Garda)** – This natural thermal park, located in Lazise, is an oasis of relaxation surrounded by lush greenery. The park features warm thermal lakes, whirlpools, and waterfalls, providing a natural spa experience in a tranquil setting. Unlike a traditional spa, visitors can soak in the open-air thermal pools at their leisure, making it a great option for those who prefer a more informal wellness retreat.

**Luxury Spa Hotels with Exclusive Treatments**
For those seeking a more exclusive spa experience, Lake Garda has several high-end hotels that specialize in wellness and relaxation. These retreats offer personalized treatments, private spa suites, and breathtaking lake views.

⇨ **Lefay Resort & Spa Lago di Garda (Gargnano)** – Perched on the hills of Gargnano, Lefay Resort is a five-star wellness retreat known for its eco-friendly philosophy and holistic spa treatments. The spa features infinity pools overlooking the lake, saltwater flotation therapy, and a range of energy-balancing treatments inspired by traditional Chinese medicine. It's an ideal choice for those looking for a luxurious escape in harmony with nature.

⇨ **Eden Reserve Hotel & Villas (Gardone Riviera)** – This exclusive retreat offers a boutique spa experience with a focus on privacy and personalized wellness. Guests can enjoy tailor-made detox programs, massages with organic essential oils, and private saunas, all while staying in elegantly designed suites and villas.

⇨ **Aqualux Hotel Spa & Suite (Bardolino)** – A modern wellness retreat in Bardolino, Aqualux is designed around water-based relaxation. The spa features multiple pools, including an outdoor heated saltwater pool, as well as saunas, steam baths, and an extensive menu of facials and body treatments.

**Boutique Wellness Centers and Holistic Escapes**
For those who prefer a more intimate and holistic approach to wellness, smaller boutique spas and wellness centers around Lake Garda provide personalized experiences.

➯ **Villa dei Campi (Gavardo)** – A hidden gem in the countryside, this eco-friendly wellness retreat focuses on natural therapies and relaxation. The outdoor bio-lake pool, herbal steam baths, and yoga sessions make it an excellent spot for those seeking a peaceful retreat away from the busier tourist areas.

➯ **Espace Chenot (L'Albereta, near Lake Iseo)** – Though technically outside the Lake Garda region, this renowned medical spa is worth mentioning for those willing to venture a bit further. Espace Chenot specializes in detoxification and anti-aging treatments using advanced wellness techniques. It attracts visitors from around the world seeking rejuvenation in a luxurious setting.

## Wellness Escapes for Rejuvenation

Beyond traditional spas, Lake Garda offers a range of wellness experiences that promote rejuvenation in natural and peaceful environments. From lakeside yoga retreats to forest bathing in the hills, the region's landscapes provide the perfect setting for relaxation and self-care.

### Yoga and Meditation Retreats

The calming presence of the lake and the surrounding mountains make Lake Garda an ideal location for yoga and meditation retreats. Several resorts and independent instructors offer sessions in peaceful outdoor settings, allowing visitors to practice mindfulness while surrounded by nature.

➯ **Yoga by the Lake (Malcesine and Bardolino)** – Many wellness centers in Malcesine and Bardolino offer guided yoga classes on the shore, where participants can practice while listening to the gentle waves. These sessions often take place at sunrise or sunset, creating a truly calming atmosphere.

➯ **Arco Yoga & Wellness Retreats** – Located near the northern tip of Lake Garda, Arco is known for its relaxed atmosphere and connection to nature. Several retreat centers here offer weekend programs that combine yoga, meditation, and healthy nutrition, making it a great option for a short wellness getaway.

➯ **Mandali Retreat Center (Lake Orta, nearby)** – Though not directly on Lake Garda, Mandali Retreat Center is a top choice for those willing to travel a bit further. This retreat offers immersive meditation programs, silent retreats, and wellness workshops in a tranquil mountain setting.

## Outdoor Wellness Activities

Rejuvenation doesn't have to be limited to indoor spas—Lake Garda's natural landscapes provide plenty of opportunities to refresh both body and mind through outdoor activities.

⇨ **Forest Bathing on Monte Baldo** – Inspired by the Japanese practice of **Shinrin-Yoku**, or forest bathing, this wellness activity involves walking slowly through the forest while engaging the senses. Monte Baldo, with its dense woodlands and fresh alpine air, is one of the best places around the lake to experience this.

⇨ **Thermal Baths and Lake Swimming** – Some visitors prefer the natural approach to wellness by taking a dip in Lake Garda's crystal-clear waters. The mineral-rich water is known to be refreshing, and in certain areas, such as Punta San Vigilio, the calm and secluded atmosphere enhances the sense of tranquility.

⇨ **Hiking for Relaxation** – Gentle hikes along the hills of Valtenesi or the olive groves of Bardolino offer a way to clear the mind while enjoying fresh air and scenic views. Several guided wellness hikes also incorporate breathing exercises and mindfulness techniques.

## Wellness Cuisine and Detox Retreats

A crucial part of any wellness escape is nourishing the body with fresh, wholesome food. Lake Garda is home to several retreats and restaurants that focus on health-conscious cuisine, using organic and locally sourced ingredients.

⇨ **Bio-Organic Restaurants** – Many restaurants in the region now offer organic, plant-based, and gluten-free menus. Places like **La Vigna (Malcesine)** and **Osteria al Cantonu (Torbole)** serve nutritious meals using fresh produce, whole grains, and olive oil from local groves.

⇨ **Detox and Fasting Programs** – Some wellness retreats around Lake Garda offer guided detox programs, including juice cleanses, fasting retreats, and nutrition workshops. These programs are often paired with spa treatments and light physical activities to support overall well-being.

For those looking to step away from the stress of daily life and focus on wellness, Lake Garda provides an ideal setting. From high-end thermal spas and holistic retreats to outdoor wellness experiences, the region offers countless ways to recharge and reconnect with both body and mind.

# CHAPTER 10: MAPS & SAMPLE ITINERARIES

## Maps for Navigating Lake Garda

Maps are an essential tool for making the most of a visit to Lake Garda. With its mix of bustling towns, peaceful villages, and diverse landscapes, understanding the region's layout can help in planning activities and choosing the best routes. Lake Garda stretches across three Italian regions—Lombardy, Veneto, and Trentino-Alto Adige—each offering distinct experiences. The northern section, framed by mountains, is ideal for outdoor activities, while the southern shores feature rolling hills, historic sites, and a relaxed atmosphere.

Well-marked roads and efficient ferry services connect the main towns, making it easy to move between destinations. However, due to the lake's size, different travel methods suit different itineraries. Driving offers flexibility, while ferries and buses are great for avoiding traffic, particularly in peak months. Cycling is also popular, especially on scenic routes along the eastern and western shores.

Tourist offices across the region provide free maps highlighting key attractions, hiking trails, and transport routes. Digital maps, such as those available through local tourism apps, offer real-time updates and suggested itineraries.

## Overview of the Region

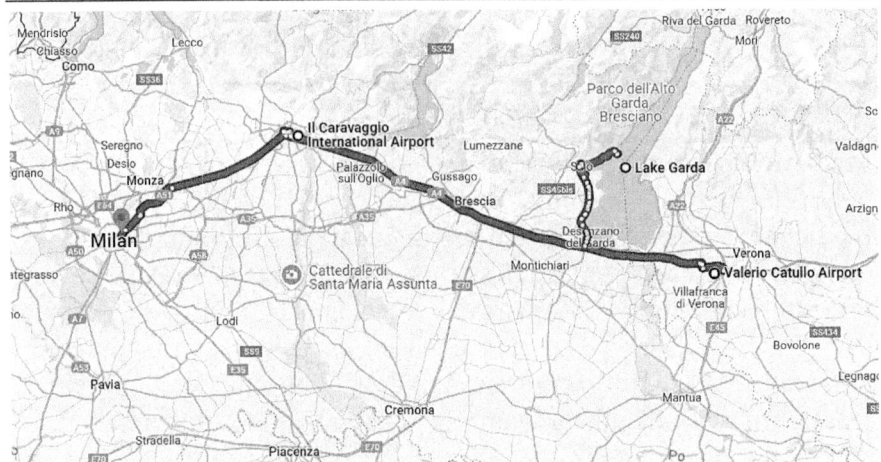

## Detailed Town Maps

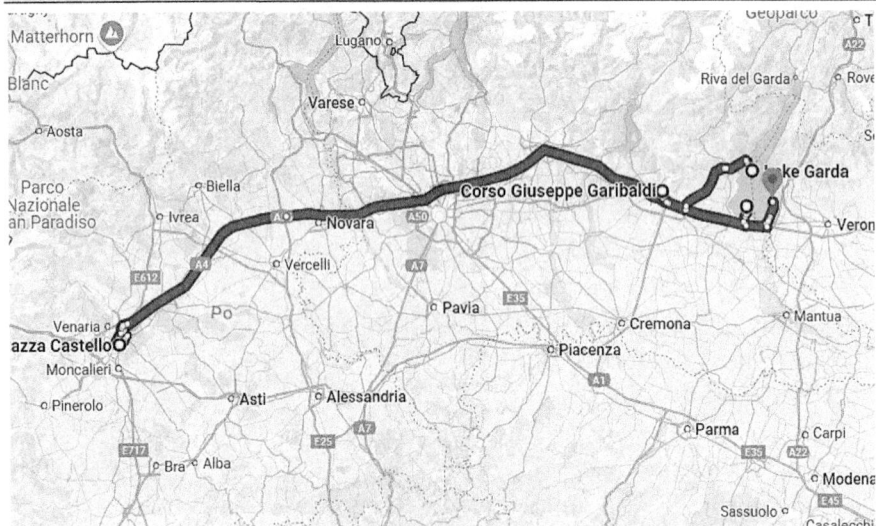

# Recommended Travel Itineraries

Lake Garda offers something for every kind of traveler, from those seeking relaxation to those craving outdoor challenges. Its varied landscape, charming towns, and mix of land and water activities make it a top destination for adventure seekers. A well-planned itinerary helps in making the most of the lake's diverse offerings, balancing high-energy pursuits with moments of rest.

For an adventurer, a week at Lake Garda can include mountain hikes, water sports, cycling routes, and even a bit of paragliding. The itinerary outlined here keeps things dynamic while allowing for some flexibility in case of weather changes or personal preferences.

## Adventurer's One-Week Plan

This itinerary is designed for travelers who love being outdoors and want to experience Lake Garda's most exciting activities. It includes hiking, cycling, water sports, and opportunities to take in the lake's best views from high above.

### Day 1: Arrival and Exploring Riva del Garda

Start the adventure in Riva del Garda, a town at the northern tip of the lake known for its dramatic mountain backdrop and active sports scene. If arriving in the afternoon, take a relaxed walk along the lakefront to get a feel for the surroundings. The old town has charming streets, and Torre Apponale offers a short climb with rewarding views. For those with extra energy, a quick hike up to Bastione, the historic fort overlooking Riva, provides a great sunset view. There's even a panoramic elevator for those wanting to save their legs for the bigger hikes ahead. End the day with a meal at one of the lakefront restaurants, refueling for the active week ahead.

### Day 2: Hiking to the Summit of Monte Altissimo

The first full day begins with one of the best hikes in the region: the climb to Monte Altissimo. This route offers incredible views of Lake Garda and the surrounding mountains. The hike can be started from the town of Nago or from Rifugio Graziani, which shortens the ascent.

The well-marked trail winds through alpine meadows and rocky paths, leading to the summit at 2,079 meters. From the top, the entire length of Lake Garda stretches out below, a breathtaking reward after the effort. The descent follows the same route or, for a change of scenery, can be done through the less-traveled forest paths leading back toward Nago.

After the hike, relax in Torbole, a small town just south of Riva del Garda. Its laid-back atmosphere and lakeside cafes are a perfect place to unwind.

### Day 3: Windsurfing or Kitesurfing in Torbole

Lake Garda's northern end is famous for its wind conditions, making it one of Europe's best spots for windsurfing and kitesurfing. Torbole has several rental shops and schools, making it easy for both beginners and experienced riders to get out on the water.

Morning sessions are usually calmer, perfect for learning, while the afternoon brings stronger winds for more experienced windsurfers. Many schools offer three-hour lessons, which are enough to get a good feel for the sport.

For those preferring a more relaxed option, stand-up paddleboarding is another great way to experience the lake's northern shores. The clear water and mountain reflections make for an incredible experience, especially early in the morning before the wind picks up.

### Day 4: Cycling the Ponale Road and Ledro Valley

One of the most scenic cycling routes in the region is the Ponale Road, a historic path carved into the cliffs above Lake Garda. Starting in Riva del Garda, this route winds up toward Lake Ledro, passing through tunnels and offering stunning views over the water.

The ride is moderate in difficulty, with a steady incline that rewards cyclists with breathtaking scenery. Once at Lake Ledro, there are options to extend the ride around the lake or even stop for a swim before heading back down.

For those wanting a bigger challenge, continuing into the remote Tremalzo Pass offers a serious test of endurance with high-altitude roads and unforgettable mountain scenery.

## Day 5: Via Ferrata Climbing in Arco

Lake Garda's northern region is a paradise for climbers, and via ferrata routes offer an exciting way to scale the cliffs with added safety. Arco, a short distance from Riva del Garda, is known as a climbing hub and has routes suited for various skill levels.

The Ferrata Colodri is a good starting point for those new to this type of climbing. It combines easy rock scrambles with sections of metal rungs and cables, leading to a rewarding viewpoint over the Sarca Valley. More experienced climbers can try the Ferrata Che Guevara, a challenging ascent that requires stamina and a head for heights.

After a morning of climbing, a visit to Arco's historic town center is a great way to wind down. The castle ruins above the town offer yet another panoramic view for those with energy left for a short hike.

## Day 6: Paragliding from Monte Baldo

After days of climbing and cycling, it's time to experience Lake Garda from above. Monte Baldo, on the eastern shore, is one of the best spots for paragliding in northern Italy. Tandem flights are available for those without experience, offering a thrilling yet smooth ride down toward Malcesine.

The Monte Baldo cable car provides an easy way to the launch site, making it accessible for everyone. Flights typically last 20–30 minutes, depending on wind conditions, and offer a completely different perspective of the lake and surrounding mountains.

For those preferring to stay on solid ground, Monte Baldo has excellent hiking trails with ridge-top views. The route from the cable car station toward Cima delle Pozzette is a rewarding alternative.

## Day 7: Relaxed Morning and Departure

After six days of high-energy activities, the final morning can be spent enjoying a slower pace. A boat ride from Malcesine to Limone sul Garda provides a relaxing way to see the lake one last time, while a morning coffee in a lakeside café makes for a peaceful ending to the adventure.

Those with extra time can take a final dip in the lake or visit one of the local markets before heading to their departure point.

# CHAPTER 11: ADDITIONAL GUIDE INFORMATION

Lake Garda's diverse landscapes, rich history, and culinary traditions make it a destination that rewards travelers who go beyond the typical tourist experience. While independent travel has its advantages, certain services can enhance a visit, offering deeper insights and unique moments that would be difficult to arrange alone. From hiring a knowledgeable guide to experiencing a private chef's creations, these options allow travelers to experience the lake in a more personalized way.

## Finding a Knowledgeable Tour Guide

Lake Garda's rich history, diverse landscapes, and cultural depth make it a fascinating place to explore with the right guidance. While it's possible to walk through medieval streets, admire castle ruins, or hike through scenic trails alone, a knowledgeable guide brings an extra dimension to the experience. With the right expert, a visit to the lake becomes a story of centuries-old battles, local traditions, and hidden spots that most travelers would never discover on their own.

### Why Hire a Tour Guide?

A guide offers more than just facts; they provide context that connects different aspects of the region. The fortifications of Riva del Garda, for example, take on new significance when understood in the context of the Venetian and Austro-Hungarian rule. The olive groves in Malcesine seem more remarkable when one learns how they have been cultivated since Roman times, influenced by the unique microclimate of the lake.

Guides also help travelers experience places beyond the tourist trail. While Sirmione's Scaliger Castle and Grotte di Catullo attract large crowds, few visitors know about the tiny village of Campo di Brenzone, a nearly abandoned medieval hamlet hidden in the hills. A guide can introduce travelers to these quiet, lesser-known places and share the stories behind them.

For food and wine lovers, a guide can provide insider access to local producers. Instead of simply tasting a bottle of Lugana wine, a visit with a guide may include meeting the winemaker, walking through the vineyard, and understanding the winemaking process firsthand. The same goes for olive oil tastings, cheese farms, and even honey producers.

### Types of Guides Available
Lake Garda has guides specializing in different areas, allowing travelers to choose an experience that best matches their interests.

➡ **Historical Guides:** These experts focus on the region's castles, churches, and archaeological sites. They explain the strategic importance of fortifications like Castello di Malcesine and recount the Roman history of towns such as Sirmione.

➡ **Nature and Hiking Guides:** For those who want to explore the trails of Monte Baldo or the waterfalls near Riva del Garda, a guide can point out unique flora, wildlife, and geological features while ensuring safe routes.

➡ **Food and Wine Guides:** These guides specialize in culinary tours, from market visits and traditional trattorias to vineyard tours and olive oil tastings.

➡ **Boat Tour Guides:** Exploring the lake by boat provides a different perspective, and guides on private boat tours share stories about the villas along the shoreline, the islands of the lake, and historical events that shaped the region.

### Where to Find a Good Guide
Finding a high-quality guide requires a bit of research. Licensed guides, particularly those affiliated with local tourism boards or professional associations, often have extensive training in history, culture, and languages. Many operate independently, while others work with tour companies offering private or small-group experiences.

➡ **Local Tourism Offices:** The official tourism boards of towns like Desenzano, Malcesine, and Riva del Garda provide recommendations for licensed guides who specialize in different areas.

➡ **Specialized Tour Companies:** Many companies focus on private or themed tours, such as food and wine experiences, archaeological excursions, or outdoor adventures.

➡ **Hotel Recommendations:** Many high-end hotels collaborate with reliable guides and can arrange personalized tours for guests.

➡ **Online Reviews and Travel Forums:** Websites like TripAdvisor and GetYourGuide feature customer reviews and ratings that help in selecting a trustworthy guide.

### Private vs. Group Tours

Both private and group tours have their advantages. Private tours allow for a flexible schedule, personalized focus, and a more in-depth experience. They are ideal for families, couples, or small groups with specific interests. A private guide can adjust the tour based on preferences, such as spending more time at a particular site or incorporating a food stop along the way.

Group tours, on the other hand, are more budget-friendly and offer a social experience where travelers can meet others. These tours follow a fixed itinerary and are usually led by guides with broad expertise, covering general history and cultural highlights.

### Tips for Hiring a Guide

➡ Check Credentials: A certified guide will have a license issued by regional tourism authorities, ensuring a level of knowledge and professionalism.

➡ Specify Interests: Whether it's history, food, or outdoor activities, letting the guide know your preferences in advance helps tailor the experience.

➡ Book in Advance: During peak season, the best guides get booked quickly. Reserving a tour ahead of time ensures availability.

➡ Ask About Language Options: Many guides speak English, German, and other languages, but it's always good to confirm in advance.

➡ Look for Guides Who Engage, Not Just Recite Facts: A great guide doesn't just list dates and names but tells engaging stories that bring the past and present to life.

➡ With the right guide, a visit to Lake Garda becomes more than just sightseeing—it becomes an experience filled with local knowledge, history, and personal discoveries.

# Enjoying a Private Chef Experience

Dining at Lake Garda is a journey through fresh ingredients, centuries-old culinary traditions, and an appreciation for slow, thoughtful preparation. While restaurants and trattorias across the region serve incredible meals, a private chef experience takes it a step further. Whether in a rented villa overlooking the lake, a cozy countryside farmhouse, or even a modern apartment, having a chef cook a personalized meal brings a new level of enjoyment to an Italian getaway.

### Why Hire a Private Chef?

A private chef offers more than just a meal—it's an opportunity to enjoy a fully customized dining experience without the hassle of making reservations, waiting for a table, or dealing with crowded restaurants. A chef focuses on personal preferences, dietary needs, and specific cravings, ensuring that every dish is made exactly as desired. For those traveling in a group, hiring a chef can be a practical option. Instead of splitting up into multiple tables at a restaurant, everyone can gather in a private setting, enjoying a meal tailored to the occasion. Whether it's a romantic dinner for two, a family celebration, or a gathering of friends, the experience feels exclusive and relaxed.

A chef also brings a deeper connection to local cuisine. Many chefs in the Lake Garda region source ingredients directly from nearby markets, farms, and specialty shops, allowing guests to enjoy dishes that reflect the freshest seasonal produce. Some even take guests on market tours beforehand, offering insight into the selection of ingredients and the importance of local sourcing.

### Types of Private Chef Experiences

➡ **Traditional Italian Dinner:** Featuring classic dishes such as handmade pasta, slow-cooked risottos, and locally sourced meats or fish, this experience highlights authentic flavors from the region.

*159*

➪ **Seafood Feast:** Given the lake's proximity to the Adriatic and the availability of fresh lake fish, a seafood-focused meal may include grilled trout, sardines from Lake Garda, or risotto al pesce persico (perch risotto).

➪ **Wine-Paired Dinner:** Some chefs collaborate with local sommeliers or have extensive wine knowledge, curating a menu where each course is paired with regional wines such as Lugana, Bardolino, or Amarone.

➪ **Cooking Class & Dinner:** For those who want to be part of the process, many chefs offer interactive experiences, teaching guests how to make pasta from scratch, knead focaccia, or prepare classic Italian sauces.

## How to Find a Private Chef

➪ **Luxury Villas & Accommodations:** Many high-end villas have a network of chefs available for hire. Some even include chef services as part of their rental package.

➪ **Local Recommendations:** Asking at wineries, specialty food shops, or even high-end restaurants can lead to great personal recommendations.

➪ **Online Platforms:** Websites such as Eatwith, Take a Chef, and CookinItaly specialize in connecting travelers with local chefs offering private dining experiences.

## Recommended Private Chefs and Services in Lake Garda

➪ **The Lake Garda Villa Company:** This company offers private chef experiences in holiday villas, providing services ranging from brunch to dinner parties. Their team includes chefs like Ada Spazzini, Jo Cooking, Mahara & Manuel, and Chef Pasquale, who is also a pâtissier at the Grand Hotel Fasano.

➪ **Igor the Private Chef:** Igor provides a complete culinary experience, preparing favorite dishes in the comfort of your accommodation. Guests have the opportunity to observe, ask questions, and even participate in the cooking process.

➪ **The Italian Elixir:** Led by Chef Anthony, this service offers private dining experiences in Verona and Lake Garda. Each menu is tailored to guests' tastes and dietary preferences, ensuring a personalized culinary journey.

➪ **Holiday Garda:** Chefs Mahara and Manuel provide in-villa dining experiences, focusing on local Lake Garda cuisine. Their services include top selections of meat and cheese, creating a complete gastronomic experience.

➪ **ChefMaison:** This platform connects guests with private chefs in Sirmione and Riva del Garda. With a network of over 1,000 chefs worldwide, they offer diverse cuisines and personalized menus, allowing guests to design their dream dining experience.

➪ **Ambra Marca:** A private chef and catering service operating in Brescia, Lake Garda, Verona, and Trento. Ambra is a member of the Italian National Chefs Team and offers personalized culinary services for various events.

**What to Expect from the Experience**

Once booked, the chef typically consults with guests to discuss dietary preferences, menu options, and any special requests. Some chefs bring all the ingredients, while others may shop with the guests at local markets before preparing the meal.

Meals are usually multi-course, starting with an antipasto such as bruschetta, cured meats, or lake fish carpaccio. The first course might include homemade pasta, risotto, or a soup, followed by a main dish featuring meat or fish. Desserts such as tiramisu or torta di mele (apple cake) often complete the meal.

Many chefs also offer wine-pairing suggestions, and some can bring bottles directly from local wineries. The experience is typically relaxed, allowing guests to enjoy the food, the company, and the setting without the rush of a traditional restaurant service.

# Car Rental Services for Easy Travel

Renting a car is one of the best ways to explore Lake Garda at your own pace. While public transportation, including trains, ferries, and buses, is efficient, having a car provides greater flexibility, especially for reaching remote villages, scenic viewpoints, and wineries that are not easily accessible otherwise.

Driving around Lake Garda offers stunning views, and the well-maintained roads make for an enjoyable experience. However, understanding rental procedures, local driving laws, and parking options is essential to avoid unnecessary stress. Below is a comprehensive guide covering everything you need to know about renting and driving a car in the Lake Garda region.

**Where to Rent a Car**

Car rental services are widely available in major cities and towns near Lake Garda, particularly in transportation hubs such as airports and train stations. Here are the best locations to pick up a rental:

**1. Airports:**

⇨ Verona Villafranca Airport (VRN) – The most convenient airport for travelers heading to the southern and eastern shores of Lake Garda. Major rental companies have offices here, making it easy to pick up a vehicle upon arrival.

⇨ Milan Malpensa (MXP) & Milan Linate (LIN) – If you're flying into Milan, you can rent a car at these airports and drive to Lake Garda in about 2 hours.

⇨ Bergamo Orio al Serio (BGY) – A good option for budget travelers arriving via Ryanair or other low-cost airlines. The airport has multiple rental agencies.

**2. Train Stations:**

⇨ Verona Porta Nuova Station – A common pickup point for travelers arriving by train from Venice, Milan, or Rome.

⇨ Brescia Station – Convenient for those exploring the western shores of Lake Garda.

⇨ Desenzano del Garda and Peschiera del Garda Stations – Smaller stations near the lake where rental agencies have offices.

**3. City Centers:**

Rental agencies also operate in town centers in places like Riva del Garda, Sirmione, and Desenzano, but availability may be more limited than at airports or train stations.

Major car rental companies operating in the region include:

⇨ Hertz

⇨ Avis

⇨ Europcar

⇨ Sixt
⇨ Budget
⇨ Enterprise
⇨ Local agencies (which may offer competitive rates but require more research into customer reviews).

## Rental Requirements and Costs

Renting a car in Italy requires meeting specific conditions. Here's what you need to know:

### Age Requirements:

⇨ The minimum age to rent a car in Italy is **18 years**, but many companies set the minimum at **21 or 23 years** for certain vehicle categories.
⇨ Drivers under **25 years old** may have to pay a "young driver" surcharge.

### License Requirements:

⇨ An **EU driver's license** is accepted without restrictions.
⇨ **Non-EU visitors** (including travelers from the US, Canada, UK, and Australia) typically need an **International Driving Permit (IDP)** alongside their national license. Italian law requires the IDP, even if some rental companies don't always ask for it at pickup.

### Credit Card Policy:

⇨ A **credit card in the driver's name** is required for the security deposit. Debit cards are usually not accepted.
⇨ Be aware of **pre-authorization holds** placed on your credit card for insurance and damages, which can range from **€500 to €1,500**, depending on the car type.

### Rental Costs:

⇨ Basic rental rates for economy cars start at **€30–€50 per day**, with discounts for weekly rentals.
⇨ Premium or larger vehicles (SUVs, convertibles, or automatic transmission cars) can cost **€80–€150 per day**.
⇨ Automatic cars are more expensive and often sell out quickly, so book in advance if you need one.

## Insurance:

➡ **Basic insurance (CDW - Collision Damage Waiver) is included**, but it comes with a high deductible.

➡ Consider purchasing **Super CDW or excess insurance** to reduce financial liability in case of an accident.

➡ Some credit cards offer rental car insurance as a benefit, but check the terms before relying on it.

## Driving Around Lake Garda

### Road Conditions:

➡ Roads around the lake are well-paved and maintained, but some are narrow, especially on the western shore where cliffs hug the roadway.

➡ Expect winding roads, particularly near Malcesine, Limone sul Garda, and Tremosine.

### Speed Limits:

➡ Urban areas: 50 km/h (31 mph)

➡ Secondary roads: 90 km/h (56 mph)

➡ Highways (Autostrada): 130 km/h (81 mph) (toll roads)

Speeding fines are strictly enforced, and many areas use automatic speed cameras.

### ZTL Zones (Limited Traffic Zones):

➡ Many historic centers, including Sirmione, Riva del Garda, and Malcesine, have restricted areas where only residents and authorized vehicles can enter.

➡ Entering a ZTL without permission results in an automatic fine, which rental companies will pass on to you.

### Toll Roads:

➡ Major highways leading to Lake Garda, such as the A4 (Milan-Venice) and A22 (Brennero-Modena), are toll roads.

➡ Payment can be made with cash, credit card, or Telepass (automatic payment device).

### Parking Options

Parking availability depends on where you are staying or visiting.

### Free Parking:

➡ Found in small villages and some residential areas.

➪ Always check signs to ensure you are not in a resident-only zone.

**Paid Parking:**

➪ Most towns have pay-and-display parking spots, costing €1–€3 **per hour**.

➪ Larger towns like Desenzano, Sirmione, and Riva del Garda have underground parking garages with daily rates around €15–€25.

**Blue Lines:** Paid public parking. Purchase a ticket from nearby machines.

**White Lines:** Free parking areas.

**Yellow Lines:** Reserved for residents, disabled drivers, or special permits.

**Hotel Parking:**

➪ Many hotels provide free or discounted parking, but historic town centers may have limited spots.

➪ If staying in a ZTL zone, ask your hotel about guest permits.

## When Renting a Car is Beneficial

While a car isn't necessary for every traveler, it's particularly useful in these situations:

➪ Exploring small villages like Tignale, Gargnano, and Torri del Benaco, where public transport is limited.

➪ Visiting wineries in the Bardolino and Lugana regions without relying on organized tours.

➪ Driving to the Dolomites or nearby cities like Mantua or Trento.

➪ Traveling with family or a group, as renting a car can be cheaper than multiple train or ferry tickets.

For those planning to stay primarily in Peschiera del Garda, Desenzano, or Riva del Garda, where public transport and ferries are frequent, a rental car may not be necessary.

## Alternative Transport Options

If renting a car feels unnecessary, there are other ways to get around Lake Garda:

➪ Ferries – Great for scenic travel between towns like Sirmione, Malcesine, and Limone.

➪ Buses – Reliable but limited in frequency, especially in smaller towns.

➡ Trains – Connect major towns to Verona, Milan, and Venice but don't reach many lakefront villages.

➡ Bike Rentals – Ideal for shorter distances, especially on the cycling paths around the lake.

A rental car provides freedom and convenience but comes with extra costs and parking considerations. Understanding these details ensures a hassle-free experience while enjoying the beauty of Lake Garda.

# Engaging Cooking Classes with Local Experts

Experiencing the food of Lake Garda goes beyond just eating—it's about understanding the ingredients, traditions, and techniques that have shaped the region's cuisine for centuries. Cooking classes with local experts offer an opportunity to step into an Italian kitchen, learn time-honored skills, and create dishes that highlight the best of Lombardy, Veneto, and Trentino's culinary heritage.

A hands-on lesson in a farmhouse, winery, or family-run trattoria brings a deeper connection to the region, allowing travelers to carry home more than just memories—they leave with recipes, techniques, and a newfound appreciation for authentic Italian cooking.

### Why Take a Cooking Class in Lake Garda?

Cooking classes offer much more than instruction—they provide a cultural exchange, where guests learn from chefs, home cooks, and food artisans who have inherited their knowledge from generations before them. Many classes also include visits to local markets, olive oil mills, or wineries, where participants can see firsthand how ingredients are selected and prepared.

Classes cater to all skill levels, from beginners looking to master basic pasta-making to experienced cooks eager to refine their risotto techniques. Small group settings ensure personal attention, making it easy to ask questions, taste along the way, and get hands-on experience shaping dough, simmering sauces, and plating dishes like a pro.

For those seeking an authentic culinary experience, learning from a local expert brings a deeper appreciation for the passion and precision behind Italian cooking.

## Types of Cooking Classes Available

**1. Pasta and Risotto Masterclasses:** Fresh pasta is a staple of northern Italian cuisine, and learning to make it from scratch is one of the most rewarding skills to take home. Classes often cover techniques for rolling and shaping different pasta types, from delicate tagliatelle to stuffed ravioli. Since rice is also central to the region's food culture, many classes focus on perfecting risotto, a dish that requires patience and precision to achieve the perfect texture.

**2. Traditional Italian Baking:** For those with a sweet tooth, baking-focused classes introduce students to Italian desserts such as tiramisu, torta di mele (apple cake), and amaretti biscuits. These lessons highlight the use of local ingredients like almonds, honey, and citrus, emphasizing the simplicity and balance that define Italian pastries.

**3. Pizza and Wood-Fired Cooking:** A pizza-making class in Italy is an essential experience. Many classes take place in agriturismos or private homes where guests learn to work with yeast, stretch dough, and bake pizzas in traditional wood-fired ovens. These classes often include lessons on making tomato sauce, choosing the right toppings, and handling high-temperature baking.

**4. Market Tours and Ingredient Selection:** Many cooking experiences begin with a visit to a local market, where participants learn to pick the freshest ingredients, from seasonal vegetables to regional cheeses and cured meats. This allows guests to understand how Italians shop and cook with what is available rather than relying on a fixed recipe.

**5. Wine and Food Pairing Classes:** For those who love both cooking and wine, some classes incorporate guided tastings, teaching guests how to pair wines like Lugana, Bardolino, and Amarone with regional dishes. These experiences often take place at vineyards or wine estates, where participants can see the winemaking process up close.

## Recommended Cooking Classes in Lake Garda

➡ **Garda Cooking Classes with Cristina:** Cristina offers intimate, home-style cooking lessons in her kitchen near Sirmione. Classes focus on traditional dishes, including handmade pasta, fresh sauces, and desserts. Guests can enjoy the meal they've prepared with a glass of local wine.

➡ **Villa Pasini Cooking School:** Located near Desenzano, this cooking school is run by a family that has been making wine and olive oil for generations. Their classes include pasta-making, bread baking, and risotto preparation, often incorporating estate-produced olive oil.

➡ **Farmhouse Cooking in Malcesine:** This rustic experience takes place in a family-run farmhouse, where guests learn to cook traditional recipes using ingredients grown on-site. The setting is relaxed and informal, with a focus on home-cooked meals made with fresh, local produce.

➡ **Eataly Verona Cooking Classes:** While technically outside Lake Garda, Eataly Verona offers high-quality cooking workshops focusing on Venetian and Lombard specialties. These classes are ideal for those who want a professional-level culinary education.

➡ **Osteria La Miniera Cooking School:** Located in Tremosine, this cooking school specializes in mountain cuisine, teaching participants how to cook hearty dishes using local cheeses, polenta, and freshwater fish.

**What to Expect from a Cooking Class**
Most cooking experiences last between two and five hours, depending on the complexity of the menu. Many classes are held in professional kitchens, private homes, or farmhouses, creating a relaxed and welcoming atmosphere. Guests are typically provided with aprons, all necessary cooking tools, and a set menu to follow.

The chef or instructor demonstrates each step of the process, allowing participants to follow along, ask questions, and practice techniques firsthand. There is often a break to enjoy wine or snacks, making the experience as social as it is educational.

At the end of the lesson, guests sit down to enjoy the meal they've prepared, often accompanied by a glass of wine or a selection of locally made cheeses and cured meats. Some instructors provide recipe booklets or online resources, allowing guests to recreate the dishes at home.

**How to Book a Cooking Class**

Many cooking classes can be arranged through hotels, agriturismos, or local tour companies. Online platforms like Airbnb Experiences, Viator, and Cookly also list a variety of cooking workshops in the Lake Garda area. Booking in advance is recommended, especially during peak travel seasons.

For those looking for a private or custom experience, many instructors are happy to tailor classes to specific dietary preferences, group sizes, or skill levels. Some even offer at-home cooking lessons, bringing all the necessary ingredients and equipment to a rented villa or apartment. Taking a cooking class in Lake Garda is more than just an opportunity to learn—it's a way to connect with the region, appreciate its culinary heritage, and bring a taste of Italy back home.

# Wine Tasting Tours in the Region

Lake Garda is surrounded by some of Italy's most prestigious wine-producing regions, each offering distinct flavors, traditions, and tasting experiences. From the crisp white wines of Lugana to the deep, complex reds of Valpolicella, the region is a paradise for wine lovers. Many wineries provide guided tastings, vineyard tours, and opportunities to learn about winemaking from experts who have honed their craft over generations.

**Notable Wine Regions Around Lake Garda**

**1. Lugana (Southern Lake Garda):** Lugana is one of the most famous white wine regions in northern Italy, known for its mineral-rich, fresh wines made primarily from the Trebbiano di Lugana grape. The region's clay-heavy soil and temperate climate, influenced by the lake, create wines with excellent structure, bright acidity, and aging potential. Many wineries offer tastings in scenic vineyard settings, where visitors can enjoy the crisp, floral notes of Lugana wines while learning about the winemaking process.

**2. Bardolino (Eastern Lake Garda):** Bardolino is celebrated for its light, fruity red wines made from a blend of Corvina, Rondinella, and Molinara grapes. These wines are often enjoyed slightly chilled and pair well with local dishes. The region also produces Chiaretto, a refreshing rosé with delicate berry and citrus flavors. Wineries in

Bardolino often include tastings with cheese and charcuterie pairings, providing a well-rounded experience.

**3. Valpolicella (Northeast of Lake Garda):** Just a short drive from Lake Garda, Valpolicella is home to some of Italy's most renowned red wines. This region produces a range of styles, from the easy-drinking Valpolicella Classico to the powerful and complex Amarone della Valpolicella, which is made using the appassimento method, where grapes are partially dried before fermentation. Many wineries offer in-depth tours that explore the unique aging techniques and provide tastings of different vintages.

**4. Franciacorta (West of Lake Garda):** For those who appreciate sparkling wines, Franciacorta is the premier destination. Unlike the more widely known Prosecco, Franciacorta is made using the traditional method, similar to Champagne, resulting in a more refined and complex wine. Wineries in the area offer guided tastings of different styles, from brut to satèn, showcasing the elegance of these sparkling wines.

### Top Wineries for Wine Tastings

**1. Ca' dei Frati (Lugana):** One of the most well-known wineries in the region, Ca' dei Frati produces some of the best Lugana wines. Their tastings include a selection of whites, reds, and sparkling wines, all served with an explanation of the estate's history and production methods.

**2. Zenato (Lugana & Valpolicella):** This family-run winery is a great choice for those who want to experience both Lugana whites and Valpolicella reds. Their guided tastings provide insight into how terroir influences the distinct characteristics of each wine.

**3. Guerrieri Rizzardi (Bardolino & Valpolicella):** Offering a mix of Bardolino and Valpolicella wines, this winery is a perfect stop for those who want to explore different wine styles. The tasting room, surrounded by vineyards, adds to the experience.

**4. Allegrini (Valpolicella):** As one of the top producers of Amarone, Allegrini is a must-visit for anyone interested in bold, complex wines. Their guided tours include tastings of Amarone, Valpolicella Classico, and other estate wines, often accompanied by local food pairings.

**5. Bellavista (Franciacorta):** For sparkling wine lovers, Bellavista offers an elegant tasting experience with their metodo classico wines. Visitors can sample different styles while learning about the meticulous production process.

**6. Zeni (Bardolino):** This winery includes a small wine museum, making it a great stop for those interested in the history of winemaking in the region. Their tastings cover a range of Bardolino wines, including red, rosé, and sparkling varieties.

## What to Expect on a Wine Tasting Tour

A wine tasting tour at Lake Garda typically includes:

➪ A guided walk through the vineyards, where you'll learn about the grape varieties and growing conditions unique to the region.

➪ A visit to the wine cellar, where winemakers explain the fermentation and aging processes.

➪ A tasting session featuring several wines, often accompanied by local cheeses, cured meats, or bread.

➪ An opportunity to purchase bottles directly from the winery, sometimes with special discounts for visitors.

Many wineries require advance reservations, particularly for guided tours and in-depth tastings. Some smaller, family-run vineyards may have limited availability, so it's best to book ahead.

## Wine Festivals and Events

Throughout the year, Lake Garda hosts several wine festivals celebrating the region's best vintages. These events often include tastings, live music, and opportunities to meet winemakers. Some of the most popular include:

➪ **Palio del Chiaretto (Bardolino, June)** – A festival dedicated to Bardolino's signature rosé, featuring wine tastings and food pairings.

➪ **Festa dell'Uva e del Vino (Bardolino, October)** – A celebration of the grape harvest with wine tastings, food stalls, and live entertainment.

➪ **Anteprima Amarone (Verona, February)** – A prestigious event showcasing the newest releases of Amarone della Valpolicella.

**Private Wine Tours and Custom Tastings**

For those looking for a more tailored experience, several tour companies offer private wine tours. These typically include transportation, guided tastings at multiple wineries, and personalized itineraries based on individual preferences. Some luxury options even include food pairings with Michelin-starred chefs or exclusive barrel tastings with winemakers.

Many high-end hotels around Lake Garda can also arrange private wine tastings on-site, bringing the experience directly to guests in a more intimate setting.

**Practical Tips for Wine Tasting**

- Book in Advance – Many wineries require reservations, especially during peak travel seasons.
- Plan for Transportation – If you plan to visit multiple wineries, consider hiring a driver or joining a guided tour to enjoy the tastings without worry.
- Try Local Food Pairings – Many wineries offer small plates with their tastings, enhancing the experience.
- Ask Questions – Winemakers are passionate about their craft and happy to share insights about their wines.
- Respect Tasting Etiquette – Take your time with each sample and enjoy the nuances of the wine before moving on to the next.

Wine tasting at Lake Garda is more than just sipping great wines— it's an opportunity to connect with the region's history, culture, and traditions. Whether visiting a small, family-run vineyard or a well-known estate, every tasting brings a new appreciation for the craftsmanship that goes into each bottle.

# Excursions and Day Trips Beyond the Lake

While Lake Garda offers plenty to see and do, venturing beyond its shores reveals a wealth of cultural, historical, and natural attractions. From medieval cities and scenic mountain landscapes to renowned wine regions, there are numerous destinations worth exploring within a short drive. These excursions offer a deeper understanding of northern Italy's rich heritage and diverse landscapes.

**1. Verona – A City of Romance and History:** Located about 30 minutes from the eastern shores of Lake Garda, Verona is a must-visit for history lovers and romantics alike. Best known as the setting for Shakespeare's *Romeo and Juliet*, the city boasts stunning Roman ruins, medieval streets, and elegant piazzas.

**Highlights of a Day Trip to Verona:**

➯ Arena di Verona – One of Italy's best-preserved Roman amphitheaters, this impressive structure hosts world-famous opera performances in the summer.

➯ Piazza delle Erbe – A lively square surrounded by historic buildings, market stalls, and cafés, perfect for soaking up the local atmosphere.

➯ Juliet's House – Though more symbolic than historically accurate, this site draws visitors eager to see the famous balcony and leave love notes on the walls.

➯ Castelvecchio & Ponte Scaligero – A striking medieval fortress and bridge offering panoramic views of the Adige River.

➯ Shopping on Via Mazzini – For those who enjoy fashion, this elegant shopping street is lined with boutiques and designer stores.

**2. Venice – A Timeless Masterpiece:** A two-hour drive or a high-speed train ride from Lake Garda, Venice is an excellent day trip for those looking to experience its unique canals and historic charm. The city's grandeur, rich artistic heritage, and labyrinthine streets make it one of the world's most enchanting destinations.

**Must-See Attractions in Venice:**

➯ St. Mark's Square & Basilica – The heart of the city, home to stunning Byzantine mosaics and breathtaking architecture.

➯ Doge's Palace – A masterpiece of Gothic design, once the seat of Venetian power.

➯ Rialto Bridge & Grand Canal – The city's most iconic bridge, offering postcard-worthy views.

➯ Gondola or Vaporetto Ride – A quintessential experience that allows visitors to see the city from the water.

➯ Murano & Burano – Nearby islands famous for glassmaking and colorful fishermen's houses.

**3. The Dolomites – A Mountain Escape:** For nature enthusiasts, the Dolomites offer dramatic peaks, scenic hiking trails, and alpine villages just a couple of hours north of Lake Garda. This UNESCO World Heritage site is ideal for a day of outdoor adventure, stunning vistas, and fresh mountain air.

**Top Spots in the Dolomites:**

➡ Lago di Braies – A striking emerald-green lake surrounded by rugged mountain peaks.

➡ Cortina d'Ampezzo – A charming alpine town known for winter sports, luxury boutiques, and mountain cuisine.

➡ Tre Cime di Lavaredo – One of the most iconic hiking destinations, offering breathtaking views of jagged rock formations.

➡ Alpe di Siusi – Europe's largest high-altitude meadow, perfect for hiking, biking, and photography.

**4. Milan – Italy's Fashion and Cultural Capital:** Milan, located about two hours from Lake Garda, is a great option for those interested in art, fashion, and historic landmarks.

**Key Attractions in Milan:**

➡ Duomo di Milano – The city's awe-inspiring cathedral, featuring intricate gothic details and rooftop views.

➡ Galleria Vittorio Emanuele II – A stunning 19th-century shopping arcade housing high-end brands and elegant cafés.

➡ The Last Supper – Leonardo da Vinci's masterpiece, housed in the Convent of Santa Maria delle Grazie (advance booking required).

➡ Brera District – A trendy area filled with art galleries, boutiques, and cozy restaurants.

➡ Sforza Castle – A Renaissance fortress with fascinating museums and lush gardens.

**5. Franciacorta – Italy's Premier Sparkling Wine Region:** For wine lovers, Franciacorta offers a more exclusive experience compared to Prosecco, producing top-tier sparkling wines using the traditional method. Located west of Lake Garda, this region is home to rolling vineyards and prestigious wineries.

**What to Expect in Franciacorta:**

➪ Guided Wine Tastings – Many wineries offer tours where visitors can sample brut, satèn, and rosé varieties.

➪ Food and Wine Pairings – Some estates offer gourmet lunches featuring local specialties paired with Franciacorta wines.

➪ Scenic Cycling Routes – The region has dedicated cycling paths that pass through vineyards and charming villages.

➪ Wine Festivals – The Franciacorta Festival, held in September, is a great time to visit for special tastings and events.

**6. Mantua – A Renaissance Gem:** Just an hour's drive south of Lake Garda, Mantua is a city steeped in Renaissance art and history. Once the seat of the powerful Gonzaga family, it remains one of Italy's best-kept secrets.

**Top Things to See in Mantua:**

➪ Palazzo Ducale – A grand palace with stunning frescoes by Mantegna.

➪ Teatro Bibiena – An intimate baroque theater where Mozart performed as a teenager.

➪ Palazzo Te – A masterpiece of Mannerist architecture, famous for its illusionistic frescoes.

➪ Lago di Mezzo – A peaceful lake surrounding the city, offering beautiful walking paths and boat tours.

**7. Sigurtà Garden Park – A Botanical Wonderland:** For a more relaxing excursion, Sigurtà Garden Park is a beautiful destination located near Valeggio sul Mincio. Covering over 600,000 square meters, it features landscaped gardens, flowering meadows, and shaded pathways.

**Highlights of Sigurtà Garden Park:**

➪ Tulip Gardens – In spring, the park is filled with vibrant tulip blooms.

➪ The Great Lawn – A vast green space perfect for picnics and leisurely walks.

➪ Medicinal Herb Garden – Showcasing plants historically used for healing purposes.

➪ Labyrinth Maze – A fun challenge for visitors of all ages.

## Practical Tips for Day Trips

➪ Transportation – Renting a car provides flexibility, especially for mountain and countryside trips. High-speed trains connect Lake Garda to major cities like Milan, Venice, and Verona.

➪ Timing – To make the most of your trip, start early in the morning and plan for possible return traffic in the evening.

➪ Advance Bookings – Some attractions, like *The Last Supper* in Milan or opera performances in Verona, require reservations well in advance.

➪ Local Cuisine – Each destination has its specialties. Try risotto all'Amarone in Verona, cicchetti in Venice, or cotoletta alla Milanese in Milan.

From historic cities and artistic treasures to alpine escapes and wine country, the areas surrounding Lake Garda offer incredible variety. Taking a day trip allows visitors to experience different facets of northern Italy while returning to the tranquility of the lake in the evening.

# APPENDICES

Traveling to a new destination is always an exciting experience, but knowing where to turn for information and assistance can make a significant difference in ensuring a smooth trip. Lake Garda is a welcoming destination with well-established services for tourists, from emergency contacts to medical facilities and visitor information centers. Having these details on hand can help travelers feel prepared for any situation.

## Important Contacts for Travelers

Lake Garda spans multiple regions—Lombardy, Veneto, and Trentino-Alto Adige—each with its own local services. While Italy's national emergency number system is consistent across the country, understanding the specifics of the area can be beneficial. Below is a comprehensive list of essential contacts for travelers visiting the lake and its surrounding towns.

### Emergency and Safety Numbers

In case of an emergency, Italy has a unified number—112—which connects callers to emergency services. However, other direct numbers exist for specific needs.

- **General Emergency (European-wide) – 112**
- **Ambulance (Medical Emergency) – 118**
- **Fire Department – 115**
- **Police (Carabinieri – National Police) – 112**
- **Local Police (Polizia Locale – Municipal Law Enforcement)** – Varies by town; found at tourism offices or local websites
- **Coast Guard (for lake emergencies) – 1530**
- **Roadside Assistance (ACI – Automobile Club d'Italia) – 803 116**

These numbers work across Italy, and operators are generally able to assist in multiple languages. In tourist-heavy areas like Lake Garda, English-speaking assistance is more common. If calling from a mobile phone, 112 automatically connects to the nearest emergency center.

For non-emergency assistance, local police stations in towns such as Desenzano del Garda, Riva del Garda, and Bardolino can provide help with lost items, minor incidents, and general safety concerns.

## Tourism Information Offices

Tourism offices around Lake Garda offer maps, event schedules, guided tour recommendations, and practical advice. Staff are typically multilingual and can assist with transport inquiries, accommodation recommendations, and local regulations.

Below are the main tourism offices around the lake:

⇨ **Desenzano del Garda Tourist Office**
  ○ Address: Via Porto Vecchio, 34, Desenzano del Garda
  ○ Phone: +39 030 374 8726
  ○ Services: Local attractions, ferry schedules, cultural events

⇨ **Sirmione Tourist Information Center**
  ○ Address: Piazzale Porto, 1, Sirmione
  ○ Phone: +39 030 990 5890
  ○ Services: Information on the Scaliger Castle, thermal baths, and historical sites

⇨ **Riva del Garda Visitor Center**
  ○ Address: Largo Medaglie d'Oro, 5, Riva del Garda
  ○ Phone: +39 0464 554 444
  ○ Services: Hiking routes, boat tours, adventure sports guidance

⇨ **Bardolino Tourist Office**
  ○ Address: Piazza Matteotti, 8, Bardolino
  ○ Phone: +39 045 621 2586
  ○ Services: Wine routes, food tastings, market days

⇨ **Malcesine Information Center**
  ○ Address: Via Capitanato, 2, Malcesine
  ○ Phone: +39 045 740 0044
  ○ Services: Cable car details for Monte Baldo, outdoor activities, local events

⇨ **Peschiera del Garda Tourism Office**
  ○ Address: Viale Stazione, Peschiera del Garda

- ○ Phone: +39 045 755 0810
- ○ Services: Information on amusement parks, cycling paths, historical tours

Each office provides printed guides, bus timetables, ferry schedules, and local insights. During peak season, visiting in the morning can help avoid long wait times.

## Nearby Medical Facilities

Health services around Lake Garda are well-developed, with hospitals, urgent care centers, and pharmacies available in all major towns. Many facilities have English-speaking staff, especially in larger hospitals.

**Hospitals & Emergency Rooms**

⇨ **Ospedale di Desenzano del Garda (Main hospital for the southern lake area)**
- ○ Address: Via A. Zatti, 1, Desenzano del Garda
- ○ Emergency Room: 24/7
- ○ Phone: +39 030 91451

⇨ **Ospedale di Peschiera del Garda**
- ○ Address: Via Monte Baldo, 24, Peschiera del Garda
- ○ Emergency Room: 24/7
- ○ Phone: +39 045 644 9111

⇨ **Ospedale di Rovereto (For travelers in the northern lake region)**
- ○ Address: Corso Verona, 4, Rovereto
- ○ Emergency Room: 24/7
- ○ Phone: +39 0464 4031

⇨ **Ospedale Santa Chiara (Trento)**
- ○ Address: Largo Medaglie d'Oro, 9, Trento
- ○ Emergency Room: 24/7
- ○ Phone: +39 0461 903111

## Urgent Care & Medical Clinics

For minor injuries, non-critical illnesses, or medical consultations, urgent care centers and private clinics provide faster assistance than hospitals.

⇨ **Garda Medica (Urgent care for tourists – summer only)**
   - o Locations: Various around the lake
   - o Availability: Seasonal, June-September
   - o Service: Walk-in consultations for minor medical needs
   - o Phone: +39 848 448 818

⇨ **Centro Medico Specialistico Desenzano**
   - o 🏠 Address: Via Agello, 26, Desenzano del Garda
   - o Phone: +39 030 912 0381
   - o Services: General practitioners, specialists, minor treatments

⇨ **Poliambulatorio San Martino (Peschiera del Garda)**
   - o 🏠 Address: Via San Martino, 4, Peschiera del Garda
   - o Phone: +39 045 640 1533
   - o Services: Private medical consultations, diagnostic tests

## Pharmacies

Pharmacies (**farmacie**) in Italy provide both prescription and over-the-counter medications, with pharmacists offering guidance on common ailments. Most towns have at least one pharmacy open 24 hours or with extended night shifts.

⇨ **Farmacia Comunale Desenzano**
   - o 🏠 Address: Via G. Marconi, 50, Desenzano del Garda
   - o Phone: +39 030 991 2170
   - o 24-hour service: Yes

⇨ **Farmacia Centrale Sirmione**
   - o 🏠 Address: Viale Guglielmo Marconi, 13, Sirmione
   - o Phone: +39 030 990 5365
   - o Late-night service: Yes

⇨ **Farmacia Madonna della Corona (Bardolino)**
   - o 🏠 Address: Via San Martino, 14, Bardolino
   - o Phone: +39 045 621 2054
   - o Late-night service: Limited

Pharmacy signs feature a green cross, and many display operating hours on their doors. If a specific pharmacy is closed, a posted sign will indicate the nearest open location.

For travelers who need prescriptions, carrying a copy of the original prescription in English or Italian can help in obtaining medications. Pharmacies do not sell strong painkillers or antibiotics without a doctor's prescription, so consulting a clinic beforehand may be necessary.

Having key contact information readily available makes traveling around Lake Garda much more manageable. Being prepared ensures a hassle-free experience.

# Language Assistance for Visitors

Lake Garda is a fantastic destination, but like any place with a rich cultural identity, understanding the local language can make your visit much smoother. While many people working in the tourism industry speak English, especially in larger towns like Desenzano del Garda and Riva del Garda, having some basic Italian phrases at your disposal can be a game-changer. Italians appreciate the effort, and even a simple **"grazie"** (thank you) or **"buongiorno"** (good morning) can open doors to friendlier interactions.

Beyond standard Italian, the regions around Lake Garda have their own dialects and expressions, which can sometimes sound completely different from the Italian you might have studied. Each part of the lake—Lombardy, Veneto, and Trentino-Alto Adige—has linguistic nuances that reflect centuries of local history. While you don't need to master these dialects, recognizing a few key words can add an extra layer of connection to your experience.

## Common Italian Phrases for Tourists

Knowing a few key phrases can make interactions much easier, especially in restaurants, shops, and when asking for directions. Below are some useful words and sentences broken down into different situations.

## Greetings & Politeness
➡ Buongiorno – Good morning
➡ Buonasera – Good evening
➡ Ciao – Hello/Bye (informal)
➡ Arrivederci – Goodbye (formal)
➡ Per favore – Please
➡ Grazie – Thank you
➡ Prego – You're welcome / Please (depending on context)
➡ Mi scusi – Excuse me / I'm sorry (formal)
➡ Scusa – Excuse me / Sorry (informal)
➡ Posso? – May I?
➡ Non capisco – I don't understand
➡ Parla inglese? – Do you speak English?

## Dining & Ordering Food
➡ Un tavolo per due, per favore. – A table for two, please.
➡ Il menù, per favore. – The menu, please.
➡ Vorrei… – I would like…
➡ Cosa mi consiglia? – What do you recommend?
➡ Senza… (cipolla, formaggio, ecc.) – Without… (onion, cheese, etc.)
➡ Il conto, per favore. – The bill, please.
➡ Posso pagare con carta? – Can I pay by card?
➡ L'acqua naturale/gassata, per favore. – Still/sparkling water, please.

## Getting Around
➡ Dove si trova…? – Where is…?
➡ Quanto costa un biglietto per…? – How much is a ticket to…?
➡ A che ora parte il traghetto? – What time does the ferry leave?
➡ Qual è la fermata per…? – What is the stop for…?
➡ Può ripetere, per favore? – Can you repeat, please?
➡ Devo cambiare treno/autobus? – Do I have to change trains/buses?

## Shopping & Markets
➡ Quanto costa? – How much does it cost?
➡ Accettate carte di credito? – Do you accept credit cards?

• • •

➡ Avete un altro colore/misura? – Do you have another color/size?

➡ Posso provarlo/la? – Can I try it on?

➡ Solo guardo, grazie. – I'm just looking, thanks.

**Emergency & Health**

➡ Aiuto! – Help!

➡ Ho bisogno di un dottore. – I need a doctor.

➡ C'è una farmacia qui vicino? – Is there a pharmacy nearby?

➡ Sto male. – I'm sick.

➡ Mi sono perso/a. – I'm lost.

➡ Chiamate un'ambulanza! – Call an ambulance!

➡ È un'emergenza. – It's an emergency.

A small phrasebook or a translation app can also be useful, but having these basic phrases in mind will help you interact with locals and get what you need with more ease.

## Regional Dialects and Expressions

Lake Garda sits at the crossroads of three regions, each with its own dialects. These local languages have been influenced by history, with elements of German, Venetian, and Lombard speech woven into everyday conversation. While standard Italian is spoken everywhere, you might hear phrases or words that don't appear in traditional textbooks.

**Lombardy (Western Lake Garda – Desenzano, Sirmione, Salò)**

In this area, people speak a dialect related to Lombard, called **Bresciano** (from the province of Brescia). It has a distinct sound, often dropping the final vowels in words.

*Common Bresciano phrases:*

➡ **Bù fés?** – How are you? (Instead of *Come stai?*)

➡ **G'ho fam.** – I'm hungry. (Instead of *Ho fame.*)

➡ **L'è bel chi.** – It's nice here. (Instead of *È bello qui.*)

Even if you don't use them yourself, recognizing these phrases might help you follow a conversation better.

• • •

## Veneto (Eastern Lake Garda – Bardolino, Garda, Malcesine)

The Veneto region has its own dialect called **Venetian**, which is spoken widely outside of formal settings. It has a softer pronunciation compared to standard Italian, with many words ending in -o or -i rather than -e.

*Common Venetian phrases:*

⇨ **Se vedemo.** – See you later. (Instead of *Ci vediamo.*)

⇨ **Mi go magnà.** – I have eaten. (Instead of *Ho mangiato.*)

⇨ **Dove che xe…?** – Where is…? (Instead of *Dove si trova…?*)

In tourist areas, people will switch to standard Italian if they notice you don't understand, but hearing Venetian in markets or small towns is common.

## Trentino-Alto Adige (Northern Lake Garda – Riva del Garda, Torbole, Arco)

The northern part of Lake Garda has a strong Germanic influence due to its history under Austrian rule. The local dialect here, **Trentino**, blends Italian with Germanic sounds. Some older residents even speak German as their first language.

*Common Trentino phrases:*

⇨ **Va ben?** – All good? (Instead of *Tutto bene?*)

⇨ **Bon di!** – Good morning! (Instead of *Buongiorno!*)

⇨ **Gavé chel là?** – Do you have that one? (Instead of *Avete quello?*)

If you visit mountain villages in this region, you may even hear Ladin, a rare language spoken in some valleys.

## Expressions Unique to Lake Garda

Certain phrases are widely understood across the lake, reflecting the area's culture and traditions.

⇨ **L'è sempre bel al lac.** – The lake is always beautiful. (Used to express pride in Lake Garda's scenery.)

⇨ **Na brisa!** – No way! (Lombard and Trentino phrase for disbelief.)

⇨ **Xe caldo oggi!** – It's hot today! (Venetian expression, often heard in summer.)

Even if you don't pick up on every nuance, knowing a few local words can make interactions feel more personal. It also helps when deciphering casual conversations in markets, family-run trattorias, or village festivals.

Learning a new language takes time, but making an effort, even with just a few words, can make your time at Lake Garda even more enjoyable.

# Further Travel Resources

Having the right resources at your fingertips can enhance your experience at Lake Garda, from planning your itinerary to discovering hidden gems that aren't always listed in mainstream guides. While personal exploration is always rewarding, a well-researched book, a reliable travel website, or a handy mobile app can provide insights that might otherwise be overlooked.

Some resources focus on historical and cultural aspects, while others prioritize practical travel tips. Whether you're interested in hiking trails, food recommendations, or transportation schedules, knowing where to find accurate information can make your trip smoother and more enjoyable.

## Recommended Books and Guides

While online resources are convenient, printed travel guides and books remain valuable. They often provide deeper historical and cultural context, helping travelers appreciate the significance of the places they visit. Below are some recommended books, categorized by their focus.

**Comprehensive Travel Guides**

⇨ *Lonely Planet Italy* – While not exclusive to Lake Garda, this guide offers detailed coverage of the region, including practical travel tips, accommodation recommendations, and local insights.

⇨ *The Rough Guide to the Italian Lakes* – A solid choice for those exploring multiple lakes in northern Italy, with specific sections dedicated to Lake Garda's towns, ferry routes, and outdoor activities.

⇨ *Rick Steves Italy* – Rick Steves provides practical advice and cultural insights, with sections covering Lake Garda's highlights and nearby destinations like Verona.

## History and Culture

➡ *A Traveller's History of Italy* by Valerio Lintner – Offers an engaging overview of Italy's history, including how various historical events shaped the Lake Garda region.

➡ *Venice and the Veneto* by Lonely Planet – While focused on Venice, this guide also covers the eastern side of Lake Garda, which falls within the Veneto region.

➡ *Italian Neighbors* by Tim Parks – A witty, insightful look at daily life in northern Italy, written by a British author who lived in the region.

## Food and Wine

➡ *Italy for the Gourmet Traveler* by Fred Plotkin – A must-read for food lovers, covering regional specialties, including those found around Lake Garda.

➡ *Vino Italiano: The Regional Wines of Italy* by Joseph Bastianich and David Lynch – A deep dive into Italy's wine culture, including the famous Bardolino and Lugana wines from the Lake Garda area.

➡ *La Cucina: The Regional Cooking of Italy* – A cookbook featuring authentic recipes from different Italian regions, including Lombardy and Veneto.

## Outdoor Activities and Hiking

➡ *Walking in Italy's Val di Fassa and Val di Fiemme* by Gillian Price – While primarily focused on the Dolomites, this book includes routes near the northern part of Lake Garda.

➡ *Cycle Touring in Italy* by Ethan Gelber – Covers cycling routes, including scenic trails around the lake.

➡ *Hiking Lake Garda: The Best Trails Around the Lake* – A practical guide specifically for hiking enthusiasts looking to explore the lake's varied landscapes.

Books offer more than just logistical guidance—they provide stories, context, and depth that can make any trip more meaningful. A well-chosen guide can enhance an afternoon stroll through a lakeside village or a hike up Monte Baldo.

## Travel Websites and Mobile Apps

Technology makes traveling easier than ever, with websites and apps offering real-time information, insider tips, and essential services. Here are some of the best resources to use before and during your trip.

**Official Travel Websites**

➪ **VisitGarda.com** – The official tourism website for Lake Garda, providing details on accommodations, events, and attractions.

➪ **Italy's National Tourist Board (Italia.it)** – Offers general travel advice, visa requirements, and cultural insights.

➪ **Trenitalia.com** – Italy's main train service provider, useful for booking tickets to Desenzano, Peschiera, and other towns near the lake.

➪ **Navigazione Laghi (navigazionelaghi.it)** – The official ferry service website, offering schedules, ticket prices, and route maps for Lake Garda's ferries.

**Mobile Apps for Travel Planning**

➪ **Google Maps** – Essential for navigation, public transport routes, and finding restaurants or attractions.

➪ **Rome2Rio** – Great for comparing different transport options, including trains, buses, and ferries.

➪ **Booking.com & Airbnb** – Ideal for finding accommodation, from luxury hotels to lakeside apartments.

➪ **TheFork** – A restaurant booking app that includes user reviews and discounts at select eateries.

**Language and Communication Apps**

➪ **Google Translate** – Offers instant translation, including an offline mode for Italian.

➪ **Duolingo** – A good app for learning basic Italian phrases before your trip.

➪ **SayHi** – A voice translation app that helps with real-time conversations in Italian.

**Outdoor and Activity Apps**

➪ **Komoot** – Great for hiking and cycling route recommendations around Lake Garda.

➪ **AllTrails** – Provides detailed trail maps, difficulty ratings, and user reviews for hiking spots.

➡ **Windy** – Useful for checking weather and wind conditions, especially for sailing or windsurfing.

**Cultural and Local Experience Apps**

➡ **GetYourGuide & Viator** – Platforms offering guided tours, day trips, and unique experiences in the region.

➡ **Museo & Touring Club Italiano Apps** – Provide detailed information on Italy's historical sites and museums.

➡ **Eventbrite** – Helps travelers find local events, concerts, and festivals happening during their stay.

Digital tools can simplify trip planning and enhance your experience at the lake, from finding the perfect hiking trail to securing a last-minute dinner reservation. Having a mix of guidebooks and technology ensures that you'll always have the right information when you need it.

Printed in Dunstable, United Kingdom

63762133R00107